The View From Here

Poems and Short Stories

by

Santa Barbara Authors

ISBN: 1547030585
ISBN-13: 978-1547030583

DEDICATION

To Joan Fallert

The Tireless Teacher
Who Guided our Growth for Many Years

and

To Sharon Alvarado

Our Intrepid New Workshop Leader

In Memorium

Frank Warren

CONTENTS

1   **My Earliest Memory** – Rosita Arbagey   1

2   **Cats Dancing in the Moonlight** – Grace Ferry   11

3   **He Left Today** – Mary Frink   13

4   **Honoring the Small** – Joy Ehle   15

5   **Make it to Heaven** – Barry Shulman   19

6   **Special Delivery** – Robert A Reid   21

7   **Having a Bit of Fun** – Joyce Metz   29

8   **Roger's Guitar** – Ken Rubenstein   31

9   **Steak and Onions** – Raven Wolfe   35

10 **In This Field** – Sharon Alvarado   43

11 **Living in the Past** – Mary Frink   47

12 **Neal** – Margaret Roff   49

13 **Where Does One Go?** – Barry Shulman   53

14 **The Cellist** – Mead Northrop   57

15 **Winter 2016** – Mary Frink   71

16 **A Turkey Tale** – Grace Ferry   73

17 **The Coach** – Brian Silsbury   79

18 **Who I Am** – Frank Warren   83

19 **Compassion** – Joy Ehle   87

20 **Saturday Night** – Barry Shulman ... 91

21 **Fortunado's** Revenge – Bill Livingstone ... 95

22 **Just** – Beth Thompson ... 99

23 **The Bad Day** – Robert A Reid ... 101

24 **Haiku** – Mary Frink ... 105

25 **Mankind** – Barry Shulman ... 107

26 **Summer Day** – Margaret Roff ... 111

27 **Thank God for Dogs** – Barbara Godley ... 113

28 **America's Forgotten Patients** – Sharon Alvarado ... 115

29 **Plants and Pots** – Joan E Jacobs ... 131

30 **Plein Air Painting** – Suzanne Yoast-Perko ... 133

31 **A Cloud Convention** – Barry Shulman ... 137

32 **On the Bus** – Bill Livingstone ... 139

33 **Shopping with Auntie** – Joyce Metz ... 143

34 **Katmandu** – Gerson Kumin ... 147

35 **Life's Newest Game** – Barry Shulman ... 153

36 **The FLK** – Robert A Reid ... 155

37 **In Front of Her** – Mary Frink ... 159

38 **The Pantsuit** – Joy Ehle ... 161

39	**Distraction** – Douglas Huston	167
40	**I as He / She** – Joan E Jacobs	169
41	**Broken Bread** – Barry Shulman	171
42	**China** – Anna Anderson	173
43	**White Tennis Shoes** – Barry Shulman	177
44	**The Promise** – Raven Wolfe	179
45	**It Wasn't the Fruitcake** – Joyce Metz	187
46	**My Dad** – Sharon Alvarado	189
47	**Adventures in Alaska** – John Ackerman	193
48	**The Hit Man** – Robert A Reid	201
49	**Where I'm From** – Joyce Metz	205
50	**Pear Blossom Alley** – Beth Thompson	207
51	**San Jose or "No Hablo Espanol"** – Margaret Roff	209
52	**Dwell and Reflect** – Barry Shulman	213
53	**Spring** – Gerson Kumin	215
54	**Coupon** – Frank Warren	217
55	**He Brought Me Red Roses** – Joyce Metz	219
56	**Summertime** – Suzanne Yoast-Perko	221
57	**Squabble** – Marge Sweet Livingstone	225

58 **Uncle Bu** – Raven Wolfe   227

59 **Last Year** I – Mary Frink   243

60 **Life After World War II** – Rosita Arbagey   245

61 **The Airport** – Brian Silsbury   251

62 **The Ice Truck** – Suzanne Yoast-Perko   259

63 **Fame** – Douglas Huston   261

64 **I Remember When** – Barbara Godley   263

65 **Where Do They Come From?** – Douglas Huston   265

66 **An Intrusion** – Joan E Jacobs   267

67 **Spring Cleaning** – Douglas Huston   271

68 **Christmas in Summerland** – Barbara Godley   275

69 **Out My Back Door** – Douglas Huston   279

70 **St. Valentine's Ball** – Brian Silsbury   283

71 **Mind Chatter** – Beth Thompson   291

72 **Grand Central Market** – Douglas Huston   293

73 **The Train Trip** – Bill Livingstone   297

74 **John Wayne Wears a Girdle** – Grace Ferry   303

75 **Grandfather Clause**– Frank Warren   311

76 **The Cruise from Hell** – Robert A Reid   313

    About the Authors   325

My Earliest Memory

by Rosita Arbagey

My earliest memory is of my mother's wrath. Mother dressed me every day as if I were a little princess. I wore little black patent "Mary Jane" shoes, white socks with lace and usually a blue or pink dress that she had designed and made herself. She expected me to stay that way until bedtime. If I did, I would be rewarded with hugs and kisses. Otherwise, I would be ignored.

In spite of this, I always had (and still have) an adventurous spirit, which Father encouraged. He instilled in me the love of horses and other animals. While on leave from Singapore, he had been asked to train a wild white stallion because he was known in the military to have a magic gift with animals. It was tradition that a white stallion always led the Aldershot Tattoo, the annual military exercise staged to raise money for military charities. And this was to be the stallion. It was love at first sight when I saw the stallion.

Days later, I remember Father took me to see the stable cat's kittens and told me to stay where I was until he came back. Getting bored, I wandered outside and heard the stallion's neighing. As I returned to the stable I felt the sun beating on my back as I went through the large open doors. The sun, the dampness, and the humidity reminded me somewhat of Singapore. There was a slight smell of urine and arnica hovering in the air.

The grooms had just finished their duties of cleaning out the stalls, hosing down the floors after currying the horses, walking them into the paddock, (with the exception of the stallion), and scattering fresh straw over the damp floor and in the stalls. The grooms were at their break sitting outside the tack room. I could hear the sound of voices, loud laughter, and the sound of sloshing as they filled their cups from a bucket that contained strong tea and condensed milk.

As I walked toward the stallion's stall, I felt the prick of straw in my socks and my feet slid a little on some of the damp straw. But my eyes were focused on the stallion, his beautiful white head hanging over the stall, his eyes blue but pink tinged, his long eyelashes enticing me. As I approached him, he gently bumped his chin on my head. I gave him a few strands of straw I had picked up around the food bin. Then I looked around and quickly crawled under the gate, just making it, but catching a splinter which pulled at my panties.

The stallion stood almost motionless with the exception of his eyes following me, his right hoof pawing the straw. He bent his head down to my height. He seemed like a giant white horse from a fairy tale, with a long beautiful mane and his tail tightly braided so when he was on parade, it would be brushed into waves cascading down his hocks, almost to the floor. I stroked his foreleg. It was like silk when my hand went down but coarse and prickly going upwards, a much harsher sensation than the touch of horsehair chairs I sat on in my Nana's house. I hugged his foreleg as if he were my teddy bear. But unlike the bear, his heat mingled with mine. I felt safe. The horse's mouth would come down and nuzzle my curls and with his deep breathing, my hair became damp and clung to my forehead. His breath was like a heater on warm, his mane hung over me like Rumpelstiltskin's hair. I do not know how long I stayed. It seemed like an eternity. I was just tired, happy and content.

Suddenly I heard stealthy footsteps. Apparently I had been reported missing and as I usually made for the stable, the grooms were searching for me. I heard my name being whispered, then rustling, then a face peered under the gate and whispered, "Rosita, leave the pretty 'orse, it's time for yer tea." I held on tighter. Again the voice whispered, "Come on, ducky, do it fer me, yer donst wants usen to get in trouble, do yer?" I still hung on. It seemed that I was an appendage of the horse and he was protecting me. Still more whispering, and for some reason, the horse suddenly became slightly agitated, his head shaking from side to side, his mane in motion, his nobly braided tail going back and forth. Yet the foreleg I clung to was motionless. All of a sudden, I heard Father's low melodious whistle and I felt the stallion raise his head as if to listen. I could not see Father, but I felt his presence, as did the horse. His voice became a whisper as he approached the stall. I heard the slight creak of the gate as it was opened very slowly. I felt air move as my father quietly approached me, his left hand reaching out to stroke the horse's forehead, his right hand on mine. I barely heard the words he whispered, they sounded like a chant. Although his were for me, he spoke to the stallion. "Rosita, love, it's time for Daddy to take the horse out. Take your hands slowly away from his leg and put them around my riding boot when I move it towards you." He put his body between me and the stallion while feeding him sugar cubes. I could smell the rich leather of his boot mixed with kiwi that Alfred (his batman) added to this "magic spit" when he carefully polished it to a mirror shine. "Now, darling, run home, Mummy's waiting for you. Alfred will take you." As he moved his leg, I grasped it until the groom grabbed me in what seemed like slow motion, backing me out of the stall and taking me out of the stables.

We all cheered when we saw my father and his groom leading the stallion in a halter and blinder to the training grounds. Before I left, the grooms hugged and kissed me until my face began to burn from their whiskers. I was fed chocolate and barley sugar. They said, "Bygom lass, that really gave us a scare, thart something else." From that day on, they became my guardians and protectors. I felt very special, very happy and very very dirty. I had been exchanged for sugar cubes!

Upon reaching home, Mother took Alfred in

to the kitchen for a cup of tea, cake, and an update on what had occurred. She had not talked to me since I stepped through the front door except to tell me to sit on the top of the stairs and wait for her. The atmosphere in the house had changed. I felt stifled, as if the walls were going to close in on me. My face was red and hot. When Alfred left, she dragged me into the bathroom, screaming that I had ruined my dress, smelled like a pigsty, disgraced her, and she would make sure that every one of the grooms was put on guard duty, and that above all, I had worried her to death. She dumped me   into a bathtub of hot water and scrubbed me down until I felt my skin was going to fall off, pushing my head backwards under the tap to get soap off my hair. I had to go straight to bed with no supper. From under the covers, I heard her banging things around. I had cried so hard I had no tears left, only sobs.

I learned from then on there was nothing like the wrath of my mother if she was not obeyed. This jogged my memory when I read the John

Mortimer books about Rumpole who referred to his wife as "she who must be obeyed."

When my father came home, Mother started reproaching him about his dereliction of duty. The arguing seemed to go on and on. I finally heard the door slam as Father left to go to the officers' mess. Many hours later I heard him tiptoe into the house and up to my room. He was still in his riding outfit, and I could smell horse on it and tobacco and liquor on his breath. He kissed and hugged me and said, "You gave us all a scare and you are not to do that again. You are my very brave little girl, but there are better ways of showing it without worrying Mummy. After the parade when the stallion is rested, I will put you on his back. He will remember you."

Within two days my mother went into the hospital and I was fostered out during the day where I could play rough and tumble with other children and have a ball. Father took me with him as much as he could. When Mother returned, she had reverted to being my beautiful loving mother again. I had learned a valuable lesson of survival and it stood me in good stead for the rest of my life. Not only did Father sit me on the stallion, he jumped on behind me and we trotted around the parade ground.

Up until the day Mother died, this would be one of the numerous tales she would recount to her friends, grandchildren and great grandchildren about her brave and beautiful daughter. Only I would remember the consequences. Upon chance meeting with former grooms, especially my father's batman, it was a memory they did not forget, starting with the words. "Eh lass dost tha remember?" and the tale would be told word for word in their dialect. Even today my grandchildren say to me, "Grandma, tell me the stallion story," and if I forget one portion of it, they will remind me. It has become part of our family folklore.

Cats Dancing in the Moonlight

by Grace Ferry

The cats started it all. Long and sleek with graceful tails and nimble feet they tangoed to the delight of all the creatures.

"Wait!" Called a voice from the brush. "I can dance too."

To everyone's delight a centipede, wearing fifty pairs of tiny black tap shoes, made his way to the center of the dance floor. He was marvelous. No one had ever seen such precision and rhythm. His one hundred little feet tippy tapped around the floor. He was a hit with the crowd. When he was done everyone yelled for more.

From high up in a branch came a very sweet voice. "I can't dance but I can play you a song."

It was a spider. She sat at the edge of her web and with her nimble fingers she plucked the

11

fine silver threads. "Oh, what a sweet melody," they agreed. By the end of the song all the creatures were swooning.

Four green frogs sang barber shop quartet songs and a parrot offered imitations of humans.

As the evening progressed, those with less talent offered to entertain. A brown dog offered to chase his tail and a chorus of chickens and a rooster sang songs from 'Oklahoma.'

"Bring back the cats!" The creatures all yelled. The cats returned to the dance floor, their shiny black fur brushed and slicked back. They took their positions on the floor and as the music started they leapt into each other's arms and waltzed so gracefully that the cow started to cry wishing she were more agile.

As the evening came to a close everyone was invited to get up and dance. What a sight it was. The dog chased his tail, the frogs line danced, the cows did a hula and the skunks danced cheek to cheek.

Please join us next time.

He left today
by Mary Frink

He left today
left the browns, grays, and greens
of his earth

he gathered flowers as he went
plucking bright pinks
yellows, and whites
"I'll use these later"
he smiled to himself

he moved faster now
skipping......twirling
soon he was running
he jumped, higher and higher
tall trees were his vaulting poles

"Good-bye" he laughed
as he burst through
the magnificent gravity
of his home, holding
the rainbows and rays of sparkling
sunlight he collected as he passed

he left today, but don't be sad
look up
into the night sky
into the immense, shimmering
vault of the heavens
he has woven his pinks, whites
and reds, his bits of silver
and gold
into iridescent garlands

he giggles as he stoops
to present them
with a flourish,
to the seated Cassiopeia

then on he floats
gathering shimmer as he goes
stocking up ....
.... for future millennia

for Joan

Honoring The Small
by Joy Ehle

It's kind of appropriate I link tomorrow's scary milestone in my life with a visit to a ten-acre island. Many folks commemorate big events with an African Safari or trip to Paris but long ago my priorities lingered and finally settled on smaller places and ideas. Instead of fretting about all of the big things I might have done I now appreciate every smile, helping hand and encouraging word.

Yellow Island is pointed out to me by my son, Karl, from the nine-passenger plane as we fly over the spot of land. Instead of a tiny island I see a gold and green colored leaf float- ing in Puget Sound and a long ago memory skips between my eyes and window glass. Noise from the single-engine turboprop doesn't discourage my diminutive memory. She runs and jumps into raked piles of colorful leaves, flinging bits and pieces of New England fall into brisk clean air.

My experiences have been large but the mode of transportation to get there has been quite the opposite. I don't enjoy big cities, crowds or long lines. Wild places have cast their spell over me. I prefer a canoe drifting across glassy water into hushed surroundings or the gentle sway of a sailboat anchored in an empty cove instead of a fancy stateroom in a floating city.

Our skiff speeds across the Sound from Deer Harbor on Orcas Island to Yellow Island. There are no docks or facilities and I'm anxious to find out if I will be able to go ashore. When we slide onto the beach, I sit on the bow and swing my legs over the side until my feet touch sand sprinkled with shell middens, evidence of long-ago Native American picnics. Maybe they made the journey in search of camas root that provided a nutritious staple to their diet or maybe they just needed a small place to honor their lives.

There are more than 120 native species of plants on Yellow Island. Each spring it shimmers with western buttercups, white fawn lilies, purple shooting stars, scarlet paintbrush and prickly pear cactus blooms. When The Nature Conservancy bought Yellow Island in 1980 it became part of the Conservancy's San Juan preserve system where the native species and habitat are protected for all of us.

My walking stick and I climb several steep steps until we reach a meandering path -- barely wide enough for one person. The whispering native grasses, the delicate glow of thousands of smiling buttercups, produce the same shivers in my spine I've felt in the most spiritual of nature's sites. I pause for a closer look into the eye of a fragile bloom and my little memory holds a single buttercup under her chin. "Do you like butter?" she asks. My mind wanders and I'm gently folded back into the landscape.

Karl and I follow the narrow trail down to a rough-hewn cabin, rooted in the sand. It was built from native stones and driftwood found on the beach by the first permanent residents, Lewis and Elizabeth Dodd. They bought Yellow Island in 1947. How extraordinary it must have been to live in a wildflower paradise and I envy their experience. Long before the environ- mental movement, the Dodds realized the importance of saving small gems on Earth.

I carefully make my way back down the steps to frothy bubbles lapping at the shore and cries from overhead birds. I take a deep breath of Salish Sea air. With a little assistance I climb into the boat. My young memory wearing a bow in her hair leans over a birthday cake. She is surrounded by a circle of cheering friends. If only I could hug her for a minute but instead I need her help tomorrow with my milestone — blowing out eighty twinkling candles.

If We Make It to Heaven
by Barry Shulman

If we make it to heaven
Where will we reside
Will the journey be long
Or just a short ride

Should we bring a good book
To help on the trip
Will we travel by plane
Or maybe a ship

Will the welcome be warm
Or something much less
An escort in shorts
Or maybe a dress

Will we live in a dorm
Or a room of our own
With the latest computer

Or an old telephone
Will there still be four seasons
Or just fall or spring
What sort of wardrobe
Should a newcomer bring

Who might we ask
And could someone tell
Would we wear the same shoes
If we landed in hell

So many questions
We all have inside
The only sure thing
We'll all share the ride

Special Delivery
by Robert A Reid

Norman A. Short kept his involvement with women to a minimum. Oh sure, he was married and, as a matter of fact, he and his wife Trudy were expecting a baby in just three weeks. But Norman saw birth as a function of his wife, and he had no intention of getting involved. He had paid an expensive obstetrician to stand by and there was no reason for the husband to be any closer than the waiting room.

"Come sit here with me, honey, and have a glass of wine." Trudy was sitting by the roaring fire in the stone hearth of their rustic Evergreen, Colorado home. She was on the floor with her back against the couch and a pillow under her knees, the only comfortable position she could find in these last months of pregnancy. Norman gazed at the firelight reflecting in her long brown hair and thought of how they met two years ago

21

at Vail when she was stretched out in front of the fire at the Heidelberg Inn drinking wine. The firelight on her long hair had captured him. The scene vanished from his mind when his gaze fixed on her swollen abdomen and he thought of how their lives were going to change forever in just three weeks. He gave her a perfunctory kiss and reclined beside her.

"How deep did the radio say the snow is now?" she asked.

"On my way home they said that we'd gotten over fourteen inches more. The roads were terrible."

"What's that now? Sixty inches in one week?"

"Yeah, over five feet. It's probably going to snow forever."

"Oh, your such a pessimist, Norman, drink your wine."

"Well, I just hope you don't go into labor because we'll never make it thirty miles into Denver on these roads."

"Then you'll just have to deliver the baby."

"Trudy, don't even joke about such a thing. You know I don't even want to come into the delivery room. It's between you and Dr. Walter. I may go get drunk somewhere."

Trudy's expression clouded and Norman put his arm around her and forced her head on his shoulder. He wished he hadn't been so frank and that he could get more enthusiasm for the upcoming birth and involving himself in it somehow.

All of their friends had taken the prepared-childbirth classes and some of the husbands were assisting with the delivery of their own child. The thought was abhorrent to him. He felt uncomfortable looking at Trudy in the nude when she wasn't pregnant and even more so now when she was all bent out of shape. Trudy raised her head off his shoulder and sat up sharply.

"Norm, I'm all wet! I think my water has broken."

Norman struggled to his feet. "How could that be? You're not due for three weeks."

"Relax, will you? When Dr. Walter examined me last week he said the baby was plenty big, I was dilated and it could come anytime now."

"Why didn't you tell me?"

"Because you get upset every time I mention the pregnancy."

"Oh baloney! What do we do now?"

'Well, call Dr. Walter. I think he will want us to come into the hospital."

Harry Walter, M.D. indeed was already at the hospital with three patients in labor. He took the call in the doctors' lounge and was staring in disbelief at the increasing savagery of the storm outside the window. "Yes, Mr. Short, we usually like the patients to come in right away when their membranes rupture. But I'm not sure you should try it from Evergreen in this weather. Is she having any contractions?"

There was a silence at the other end of the phone as Norman consulted with Trudy. "She says they're about seven minutes apart."

"Have you had any experience delivering

babies?"

"I'll get her there right away, doctor!"

"But the roads...you may never make..." The other end of the line was dead. Dr. Walter sighed and the furrow in his brow became a little deeper.

"What did Dr. Walter say?" Trudy asked.

"He said to come right in. Let's go."

The wind was whipping the snow across the canyon as they headed toward Denver. Because it was snowing particularly hard, the giant orange sand and plow trucks had no chance of keeping the roads clear. Norman had no confidence in the traction of the car and felt completely at the mercy of the elements. He made very small steering adjustments at twenty miles per hour, his wet palms firmly grasping the steering wheel.

Trudy's labor meanwhile appeared to be getting more active and she would quicken her breathing at ever more frequent intervals as the car poked along. Suddenly her body stiffened and she let out a short scream. Norman started, inadvertently jerked the wheel and the precariously controlled car careened into a deep snow drift at the edge of the creek bed, ten feet below the level of the road. Nobody was hurt but Trudy was hurting. "I think the baby's coming, Norm. Help me off with my pants."

"I'll go for help. Surely somebody will be passing on the road."

"Dammit Norm! There's no time for that. Do what I say!'

He helped her over the seat then crawled into the back himself. He took off his coat and covered her with it.

"There are some towels in my suitcase. Get them to wrap the baby in."

With hands shaking to the point of no control, Norman obeyed.

"Okay. Now I'm going to push down and as the head comes out you support it and help it turn the way it wants to go. Then when it's completely turned and looking at one of my legs, you pull the head gently towards the floor and the shoulder will be born. The rest will be easy.

Got that?"

There was no answer but there was no time. A tiny head covered with black hair was emerging and starting to turn toward Trudy's left leg. Norman with tears welling in his eyes and exhilaration starting to fill his chest cradled the tiny skull and pulled gently towards the floor. The shoulder cleared and he found himself with his daughter in his arms.

His excitement turned to fear, however, as he realized that she was struggling to breathe and appeared purple in color. He looked at Trudy but the reassuring confidence had left her face. Quickly he put his mouth over the baby's and gently blew until the chest seemed to expand. There was a cough and slight improvement in color, so he did it again and was rewarded with a larger cough, then a loud healthy cry. He wrapped the baby in the towels and handed her to Trudy. "Now I'll go get help."

"Norman." He could see the lingering tears in his wife's eyes and admiration on her face. Her hair was tumbling over her fur collar and onto the wad of towels in which the baby gurgled. He loved her more at that moment than he ever had and, for that matter, liked himself a little better too. "You were terrific, darling. Will you deliver all my babies for me?"

He kissed her tenderly and said. "You shush and keep my little girl warm."

Norman struggled up to the road where he was able to flag a passing motorist. Together they assisted Trudy and the baby into the car and continued gingerly down the canyon toward Denver. In the back seat Norman had taken possession of his daughter and did not relinquish her until the pediatrician at the hospital convinced him that she should be weighed, measured and have a footprint made.

Trudy was taken to the delivery room for an examination and only then did the new dad repair to the waiting room where he had planned to spend so much time.

Having a Bit of Fun While Waiting for Elise
by Joyce Metz

"Do you give samples?"

"Sorry, ma'am, I don't."

"Gee, when I was a kid the bread truck would come through our neighborhood a couple of times a week. If I asked for a sample, the driver would hand me a squashed loaf, if he had one."

"Well, I can't do that, but if you go in the store they always give out samples." He pointed toward the See's Candies Shop.

"I know that. I was just testing you."

He climbed into the back of the See's trailer truck. I could see into the dark depths where pallets of See's chocolates filled the trailer from top to bottom. Surely there must be at least one dented box in there.

Not willing to give up easily, I persisted.

"When I was a little girl there was a German bakery in our town. The owner would give me a day-old doughnut if I waited outside his back screen door, looking pitiful. Maybe you've got some out-of-date chocolates in the back of your truck?"

"Sorry, lady, you don't look pitiful enough."

Roger's Guitar
by Ken Rubenstein

Late 2015 with Christmas fast approaching. On a cloudy, cool Saturday, as I crossed the parking lot headed for the Goleta Trader Joe's, I heard a familiar voice singing with guitar accompaniment. The man I knew only as Roger has busked there twice a week for the last several months. I've often smiled and tossed a buck into his open guitar case, noting that he plays a nice looking Martin, my own favored brand. Roger appears to be in his fifties, an average looking guy with a face that suggests he's done some hard traveling.

That day something was different. He played a black guitar, and it didn't sound anywhere near as good as the Martin. I asked him what happened, and he explained that someone broke into his truck and stole the instrument. The loss was especially hard because the Martin had once belonged to his late wife. He bought the cheap replacement at Costco, and said it was like playing a rock.

I felt sad for him, surrendered a fiver, and continued on into the store. While shopping I couldn't help thinking about the three guitars I had at home: a Martin, a Cargo, and my most recent acquisition. I'd had a pretty good year financially and treated myself to an Eastman guitar, which had received some very nice reviews. It cost $800, considerably less than I'd paid for the Martin. I'd had it for about six months and, in truth, didn't play it much.

Now I'm not particularly oriented to philanthropy. You know, a buck or two here and there to homeless people, a few hundred dollars a year to worthy causes, extra stuff donated to the local thrift store charity. I'd never even come close to anything like giving away a guitar. Yet something inside wouldn't stop pestering me. He needs it, you hardly use it. What good's it doing in the closet?

After shopping, I went home, opened the case, took out the Eastman, and strummed a few chords. Sounded nice, but needed some playing time to reach its full glory. On impulse, or maybe some inner command, I carried the guitar back to TJs and showed it to Roger. He admired its look, and I asked him to play something. He did, and reported it sure beat playing a rock. I told him it was his. He didn't believe me at first, perhaps thinking it improbable that anyone would walk up and give him a nice guitar. When his shock caught up to reality, he became so effusive in his thanks that I began to feel embarrassed. We chatted a while, he played his new guitar, and we parted.

Now, a year and a half later, he still busks the TJ lot twice a week. We chat briefly most times I pass, and he's thanked me in one way or another just about every time. He reports that the

Eastman's rosewood top has opened nicely, and I hear the difference. They've bonded, he and the guitar.

Y'know, I can report unequivocally that even though he got a nice gift that Christmas, mine was even better.

Steak and Onions, Watched the Fights
by Raven Wolfe

The marble hallway in my grandparents' apartment building smells like mold and fried onions. They live in the Ritz apartments. "Mom and Dad are living down at the Ritz" my mother says to her friends. Something to brag about. For a long time I believe the Ritz is ritzy until, as an adult, I remember that behind the building garbage cans were overflowing and rats scampered away whenever anyone came out to dump their trash.

As the oldest grandchild, I am the only one ever invited to spend the night. By the time the others are old enough, my grandparents have given up having grandchildren or anyone, for that matter, visit them at home.

They live on the ground floor and the windows are flush with the street. When people walk by all we can see is their feet and legs. My grandmother, (I call her Nana), recognizes the residents by their shoes. "Here comes Sadie Nusbaum. Look at those awful brown shoes. Doesn't she know better?" My Nana wears black cutout shoes with chunky heels and straps. She is barely five feet tall with red hair and green eyes. Most of the residents at the Ritz are old Jewish women that my grandmother disdains and my grandfather charms. He is dark and sultry and loves to flirt with the women. My grandmother flutters her eyelashes when she is around men, including my grandfather. She never has time for friends or neighbors. In the early 1950s, her entire life is my grandfather and reading movie magazines. She knows everything about Marilyn Monroe and Liz Taylor.

I am allowed to spend the night only on Fridays. My mother drops me off around dinnertime, just as my grandfather comes home from working in my father's automotive supply store. The walls in the apartment are pale blue, and each time I look at them, I tell myself they are the color of the sky. Blue skies are a rare event in Canton Ohio.

I know to stay out of the kitchen, out of my Nana's way, as she cooks the only thing I ever see her prepare. Fried onions for the steak that my grandfather has to cook. They had owned a string of diners on the Atlantic City Boardwalk, where my grandfather was involved in the New Jersey mafia. My grandmother never learned to cook, as her own father had owned a restaurant in New York City.

My grandfather is short and dark and tough. Born in Romania, he and his family emigrated to the U.S in the early 1900s. He grew up on the streets of New York. He yells at drivers and gives them the finger, but with my grandmother, he is gentle and protective. Maybe it's all that eyelash fluttering.

As the air fills with the sizzling sound of steak and onions, I sit at a small desk drawing pictures on the back of a pad of bank deposit slips from the Dime's Savings Bank. My Grandfather is in the bathroom, where he spends large amounts of time, until my Nana tells him it's time to cook the steak.

My grandfather starts the meal with a shot of Canadian Club Whiskey ("Doctor's orders", he claims.) My Nana and I drink small glasses of tomato juice. We toast each other and say "L'Chiam". The three of us sit in the dark kitchen at the small linoleum table under a single window shaded by the branches of a thick bush. Outside cars drive down Sixth Street and we can see the feet of people walking by. Every once in a while my Nana will mutter something like "Where's she been all day? Oy, he's visiting her again?" Sometimes she says these things in Yiddish, but I still understand her.

After dinner my grandfather takes me behind the apartment to dump the garbage. It is a kind of ritual, our only time alone together. Behind the building we meet other residents, mostly women taking their trash to the overflowing cans. My grandfather puts his foot up on a rickety bench as he smokes and talks to these women, who pat my curls and say how big I am getting. They call me "shana madela."   Most of the time they speak Yiddish.

Eventually we head back to the apartment. He tells me to never tell my Nana who he has talked to, as if I know the names of these women. They all look alike to me - gray hair and house dresses. We climb the back fire escape to the third floor and walk through the dim echoing halls until we reach our destination - the corner right apartment on the ground floor. Sometimes my grandfather tells me who lives behind each door. Most of the names he rattles off are Mrs. So and So, as if he is the only man living at the Ritz. His deep voice echoes in the air around us.

Friday night fights are always the agenda for the evening. The air buzzes with familiar names - Rocky Marciano, Joe Louis, Sugar Ray and Jersey Joe. My grandfather puts on striped pajamas and leather slippers, except in the summer, when my Nana lets him wear boxer shorts and a cut-out undershirt.

Nana loves soft slippery nightgowns in pastel colors that gently caress her large breasts. During the boxing matches my grandfather yells and says things like "son of a bitch" until my Nana tells him to "keep it down, Harry. The neighbors can hear you." I try to match my excitement level to that of my grandfather's and wiggle around on the couch until I am told to stop fidgeting. Eventually my Nana tucks me into their double bed, where she and I will sleep while my grandfather spends the night on the couch. After my grandfather has a heart attack the sleeping arrangements change and I am relegated to the couch so he can sleep in his own bed.

In the morning my Nana and I wake up at dawn and whisper and giggle. She scratches my back and frets over my hair, asking me "where did you get these curls?" as if I had found them somewhere. We tiptoe into the kitchen, where she fixes us instant coffee and orange juice in small glasses that have the design of cherries etched along the top rim. We look at the many pictures I drew the day before. My Nana takes great interest in my artwork, exclaiming what a beautiful dog or cat or boy I have drawn. Sometimes she draws pictures for me. Her drawings aren't much better than my own six year old attempts.

After my grandfather wakes up he goes into the bathroom for one of his hour long visits. He makes strange growling noises in there. I am told he is "clearing his throat." There is a lot of coughing and hacking. That is when my mother is called to come and get me. As we drive across town, she always asks me the same questions – "What did you eat? What did you do?" The answer is always the same. "Steak and onions, watched the fights."

In This Field

by Sharon Alvarado

My Father, who never saved anything, saved this: a 4 ½ X 7 inch green soft-covered book titled: <u>United States Temporary Military Cemeteries European Theater Area World War II,</u> a pictorial,   historical record prepared by the American Graves Registration Command.

Last year my mother died. I discovered this book when I was going through their belongings, important papers and items they had saved for many years. I identified it as my father's. I recognized his handwriting.

I never saw this book before, nor had my father ever discussed it or what it meant to him. I thumb through the pages, shocked at the pictures of thousands of crosses.

The   second   page   under   the   heading

FRANCE lists 24 cemeteries. One is circled: St. Avold. There is a map of the cemetery and a brief paragraph. It states: St. Avold is situated on the eastern boundary of France; established by the Seventh U.S. Army on 16 March 1945, it is one of the last military cemeteries established in Europe and overlooks the rolling countryside across which Allied troops made their great drive toward the Rhine and final victory.

There are 15, 303 American soldiers interred in St. Avold Cemetery. This follows with four more small pictures. Next to one picture my father has written:

In this field

A man stands over the grave. He is wearing an American army uniform with a dark overcoat. His head is covered with his garrison cap, he holds something in his right hand.

Is it my father? The man has thick black hair, a dark complexion, like my dad, he is medium height, muscular. He is looking intently down at the grave.

Is it my dad or do I just imagine it?

Who is buried in this grave, so very far from home?

Why did my father save this book?

Fifty-six years it has been at the bottom of his bedside drawer.

What did he mean "in this field"?

During my childhood, I remember my father as a man without a voice. Silently standing outside the group, always and forever in the background.

My father's voice comes to me now

"In this field

In this field"

The View from Here

Living
by Mary Frink

living in the past:
she should have
he didn't
I might have

living in the future:
if only
I want
why can't

living in the moment:
the sky
the tree
the moon
the bird
the dog
the monk
the child

The View from Here

Neal

by Margaret Roff

One night a week I deliver a dinner prepared by a local restaurant to Neal, who has AIDS. Neal moved to an apartment owned by the County of Santa Barbara near Old Town Goleta. I do not know much about his life except he had a beauty salon in Loreta Plaza near the Post Office and his Vietnam partner died of AIDS.

His apartment is always clean. He has a futon in the living room which can be made into a bed and a set of plain white china dishes which are kept on shelves near his table.

Neal never mentions any family members and I don't ask. He is easy to talk to and always positive in his outlook. He said before he was ill he participated in a social, sport group sponsored by the Gay and Lesbian Resource Center.

One day when I arrive he has several friends

visiting. I can sense that they look up to Neal. He introduces me and I feel included in the group.

Another visit, when I arrived his first comment to me was, "What is wrong?"

"My sister is visiting me." I am taken aback that he could sense this. I was feeling tense.

Weeks later, I heard from one the Leaders of AIDSCAP, that Neal was found passed out in his apartment and taken to Saint Francis Hospital.

When I went to visit him, he asked "Don't you have anything better to do than visit someone in the hospital?"

I explained. "I was tired of working on my income taxes and needed something else to do."

He laughed softly and then complained about the nurses, what they did and did not do.

I said, "I am so glad you are feeling so much better. The fact that you are noticing what the nurses are doing means you are getting better."

He paused to absorb what I said and said "You are right, a few days ago I would not have noticed."

In a few days he was moved to the newly opened Heath House, a hospice for AIDS patients. Alice Heath had worked hard to find grant monies available for a hospice.

I was planning to stop to see him but was told that he had already passed away.

I attended his memorial service at Goleta Beach. There was a group of about thirty people. Neal had given a CD to a friend with a song he wanted to have played at his memorial. We gather around a car to listen to the song "Peace I Leave with you my Friend."

Where Does One Go?

by Barry Shulman

Where does one go
When one doesn't care
Put on a hat
And don't comb your hair

Raindrops are dancing
On a nearby drain
Look for a shirt
Without a big stain

Call up a friend
You know is not home
No one is there
To answer the phone

It's been two weeks now
Since I heard someone say
There's a train bound for Fresno

But it's only one way
And my cousin who lived there
Has just moved away

There's always a movie
Or Dominic's bar
But there's only six bucks
Left in my jar

Some seniors play bingo
Each Saturday night
But with only six bucks
It wouldn't be right

I've read every book
That's still on the shelf
I'm not bad to look at
And still have my health

If you know anyone
Could you give me a call
We could meet up the block

The View from Here

At the neighborhood mall
There must be another
Ask your sister or brother
With six bucks to share
I'll take off my hat
And go comb my hair

The Cellist

by Mead Northrop

The Beginning

I decided to become a cellist at age 60. I found a teacher, located a "rent to buy" beginner's instrument and began practicing diligently for my weekly lessons. I studied some piano as a child and could read music at a basic level. When I discovered that a beginning cellist only played one note at a time, I thought that following the score would be relatively straightforward.

My first pieces were played on open strings without any fingering by the left hand. I tuned the four strings: A, D, G and C, by playing them one at a time while adjusting their tension in order to get the needle on my electronic tuning device to point directly vertical, indicating the proper pitch. Eventually, I graduated to the first position – a system of fingering a string that raised its pitch in half steps from the open string tone. To assure that I placed my fingers properly, my teacher pasted strips of Scotch Tape onto the fingerboard so I could see where to position the fingers of my left hand. Eventually, when I could feel the proper placement, the tape would come off.

Our older son was going to school in Boston, having chosen medicine over a career in music. He was engaged to an accomplished pianist, with whom he shared a passion for music. The year before, he visited her family at Christmas. When he phoned home to wish us well, he said, "These people are amazing, they sit around and sight read Bach for fun."

Steeped in Germanic tradition, the family was deeply devoted to studying and performing serious music. The father played viola; the son, cello; the younger sister, violin, and the fiancé played piano. My wife and I met our son's future in-laws at their home in New Jersey six months before the upcoming wedding. We had come to choose a venue for our rehearsal dinner. The father, Peter Fritze, proudly announced that they had already planned all of the music for the ceremony. Musician relatives would perform most of it.

We identified a suitable restaurant for our rehearsal party. It was then that Peter and his wife Hildegard announced that their family had a long tradition of performing skits and songs ridiculing the bride and groom at parties on the eve of weddings, and that family musicians always played music during the cocktail hour. Peter said, "Since you play the cello, we want you to perform with us that night. It will be lots of fun to have you join in. We'll put together a program and send the scores to Santa Barbara this spring."

Fun? I played on a cheap instrument that I tuned with an electronic gizmo. It had scotch tape on the fingerboard, and I carried it about in a cheap canvas case. My career had spanned six months, and now I was expected to perform side by side with lifelong musicians at a party I was to host!

Wedding Music

The musical scores for the rehearsal dinner arrived by mail in early April. Peter Fritze, the bride's father, selected a long, lively classical Italian piece for strings, and three or four show tunes having wedding motifs like, "I'm Getting Married in the Morning," from "My Fair Lady."

As I scanned the scores, my stomach knotted. Barely able to play "Twinkle, Twinkle Little Star," I was confronted with compositions written in complex keys, fast tempos, with multiple repeats and long rests requiring perfectly timed reentries. I picked up the phone and called New Jersey. "Peter, I can't play this stuff," I said.

"What are you, a chicken?" Peter asked.

"The cello parts aren't that hard. Besides, the bride's cousin Christina will play cello with you. Christina has studied for years. We just arranged for you to borrow our son's cello teacher's instrument," Peter added proudly.

"Okay, I'll take the scores to my teacher and see what she thinks and get back to you." (Peter and I have since become close friends and admirers, but at that point we were both trying our best to remain polite.)

My teacher called it the "wedding music," and we worked on it furiously for weeks. To my surprise, I was eventually able to play it when we were a duet. Only a split-second behind her, I could get through the fast parts, change keys and count out the rest periods properly. I began to think I could pull it off.

One night in early May, I awoke in a drenching sweat. The borrowed cello wouldn't have any scotch tape on its fingerboard! How would I figure out where to position my fingers on that cello teacher's elegant instrument? "We could measure the distances, and, when you get to New Jersey, you could put some tape on his cello's fingerboard," my teacher offered.

Finally, it was time to travel. "Whatever you do, don't stop," my teacher advised me as we ended our last practice session. All I could think about on the eve of this family celebration was playing those damned pieces.

"We rehearse at 3 o'clock," Peter announced. I was carefully handed the borrowed cello. Its fingerboard was black and smooth. Our ensemble consisted of Peter, the bride's sister, two cousins and me. Cousin Christina, my fellow cellist, was missing. "We can't wait for Christina any longer. We must tune," Peter ordered.

Tune? I'd never attempted tuning without my electronic device that I'd forgotten to bring. Someone played what I assumed was an A on the piano, and I faked changing the tension of my strings. The doorbell rang. It was Christina. "I'm counting on you leading me through this," I pleaded.

"Peter has a poor memory," she announced. "I haven't played the cello for five years. Let me see the music. Wow. Some of this looks tricky."

Five years? Tricky? She planned to sight read the stuff that I'd been slaving over since April. I was doomed!

The Wolf

Our quintet wedged itself into one corner of the dining room. Peter quieted the guests and announced our rehearsal dinner program. Terrified, I barely heard Peter count, "One, two, three, four."

We began to play. I appeared to be keeping up, but I knew that I was missing notes all over the place. I even stopped once, but cousin Christina covered me. Finally, applause. It was over. My son hugged me proudly. I headed straight for the bar. Stiff drink in hand, I assumed my role as host. At dinner I welcomed everyone and made some heartfelt toasts. I thoroughly enjoyed the rest of the weekend.

Back in Santa Barbara, I continued my studies and eventually purchased a wonderful cello fashioned for me by Jim Wimmer, our local, world-renowned luthier. When properly bowed my instrument emitted rich, bold, sustained tones. I was very proud to own it. However, I could only coax my cello to produce sounds consistent with my novice status. So, when the Music Academy students arrived for the 1999 summer festival, I invited two cellists to my home to hear my prized instrument played by real musicians. As I sat there in reverie listening to one of them produce beautiful music on my treasured cello, it suddenly emitted a horrible, buzzing sound. "Whoa! What was that?" I shouted, fearing the cellist had uncovered a heretofore-unknown structural defect in my costly instrument.

"Oh, that's just a wolf," the student explained. " Most good cellos emit wolfs. A note that I played caused a sympathetic overtone to resonate in the cello's body. We call it a wolf-tone. You need to buy a wolf stopper and have your teacher attach it to the offending string. That will fix it."

The next morning, I purchased a wolf tone eliminator and headed to my teacher's house. I told her about the terrible sound my cello emitted when the Academy student played for me. "How come I've never heard that before?" I asked.

"You haven't heard that before because you can't play well enough to produce it," she said. "Since you've bought the wolf stopper, I'll install it. Then, your cello will appear even more authentic."

That fall, my teacher asked her three adult students to meet once a month for a group lesson. We performed works scored for three cellos. It was a struggle for me, but fun to play as an ensemble without the pressure of any rehearsal dinners. As December approached, we worked up a program of holiday music with the intent of giving an informal performance for family and friends. I volunteered our home as the venue for the recital. Properly tuned, we three sat in a row behind our music stands ready to play our festive program. We were a junior high school principal, a prominent local attorney and a recently retired physician.

Afterwards, the lawyer's mother-in-law, a former piano teacher visiting from Washington, D.C., whispered to my wife, "They weren't as bad as I expected."

The Piano Trio

I decided to form a piano trio. Practicing the cello had become a lonely experience. I had been at it for over four years. I wanted to make music with others, so I explored the possibility of playing as a trio with a violinist and a pianist. A newly retired friend had played violin in his high school orchestra and, inspired by me, began to take lessons. Because of his earlier teaching, he progressed rapidly. I approached him to become the violinist in my trio. Our prospective pianist was a bona fide musician. She played for her pleasure daily. An old friend and neighbor, she had a marvelous sense of humor and thought playing with two novices could be fun. She agreed to join us.

The violinist bought music for us. He selected two volumes of works arranged for beginning piano trio. The first book consisted of about twenty well-known, hummable classical melodies that had been dumbed down for ease of play. A music teacher from the Midwest had written the second book, a group of original compositions for a beginning piano trio. We met to review the scores. We chose selections from each book and agreed upon a date for our debut. The violinist and I needed several days to practice independently. Our pianist could easily sight-read such basic compositions.

It was fun to rehearse the familiar melodies. Somehow, with knowledge of how they were supposed to sound, my bow glided effortlessly across the strings. The original compositions were another matter. Lacking the skill to view a musical score and hear it in my brain, I just had to dig in and practice the work until it began to sound familiar.

Our agreed upon date arrived, and we gathered at the pianist's home eager to play. We set up in her living room beside the piano. We decided to perform the familiar pieces first. The first time through we sounded pretty good. We kept the beat, came in on time and the strings played only a few sour notes. We ran through each piece two or three times and improved with each playing.

Then, we turned to the original composition. After a couple of false starts, we began to play the unfamiliar melody. We had played several bars when the piece began to sound strident and disorganized; sort of like something avant-garde composers Alban Berg or Arnold Schoenberg might have written for a twelve-tone system. We continued for about two minutes. Then, the pianist suddenly stopped playing.

"Why did you stop? Why did you stop?" the violinist shouted.

Our accomplished pianist looked straight at both of us and declared resolutely, "I stopped because it's over."

Winter 2016
by Mary Frink

The sky is blue

the sun is warm

a hummingbird's iridescence

dances atop the Cape Honeysuckle

A weak, insecure man

spewing hatred

takes the White House

America descends

into a

deep

dark

depressed

hopeless

winter

A Turkey Tale

by Grace Ferry

My parents are not very smart people. Don't get me wrong, they're sweet, kind people who can't say no and do things which usually get them in some sort of trouble. For example, my dad was fired because he walked off his job to help his friend get his car started. My mom wound up with ten cats from a crazy lady who never came back for them. Not until the fleas had almost eaten us alive did she agree to call the pound.

When Dad comes home and tells Mom he's being fired she's doesn't get angry. She puts her hand on his shoulder, "Don't worry", she says, "you'll find a job soon, an even better one."

It's fall and school's about to start, so my parents decide that my dad has a better chance of finding work in San Antonio. We pack our few belongings in a couple of crates, load up the old car and off we go.

We find a small place to rent in the Mexican neighborhood. Right away Mom starts cleaning and by the time she's done it doesn't look half bad. I take my sister by the hand and we walk up and down the street looking in store windows. Gee, I didn't know there were so many Mexicans in San Antonio. There's the Mexican bakery, the Mexican butcher, and the store that sells bundles of dried herbs, flowers and magic potions. The store belongs to an old woman; everyone says she's a witch. I yank my sister's hand and run fast when we pass that door.

My dad goes looking for work every day. So far he hasn't found a job and my mom takes in laundry and cleans other people's houses to make money. It's almost Thanksgiving Day and in school we're coloring pictures of Pilgrims, Indians and turkeys. All the kids tell which is their favorite part of the bird.

I can't remember having turkey before but it must be like a big chicken, so when it's my turn I proudly say "the wings". The sound of "yum" from the kids makes me feel I've made a good choice although I've have no idea what they taste like.   Our family celebrates all holidays with tamales.

"Papa, can we have turkey on Thanksgiving Day? All the kids at school are
talking about how good it is and how everyone is supposed to eat turkey on Thanksgiving Day because the Indians said we have to."

My dad glances at my mom. "I had turkey once in Mexico and we cooked it in chile sauce."

"No, no Mom, that's not Thanksgiving Turkey, we need a turkey with its feet up in the air with carrots and things around it."
My dad doesn't say anything but he looks sad. He just gets up and goes outside, even though it's cold. It's two days before Thanksgiving and all I see is the usual stuff we always eat, beans, potatoes, chilies and tortillas.

I come home from school and find my mother sobbing into her apron.

"Mom!" I yell, "what's the matter."
She grabs me by the shoulders and pulls me in real close so that my little sister can't hear, "Your dad's in jail."

"In jail! Why?" I scream.

"He was caught taking a turkey from the *ranchito* by the creek. The police came and took

75

him."

"Did you keep the turkey?"
She just stares at me with squinty eyes. I know that look. It means 'shut-up.' For sure we're not having turkey or our dad on Thanksgiving Day.

The cold wind that comes from the north makes the windows rattle. We wear our coats inside the house to keep warm. The wind shakes the pecan trees and I join the other kids picking up nuts. Between my sister and me we nearly fill our sack. We sit on the floor in the kitchen and crack the pecans open with a rock and eat until our stomachs hurt.

"Pick up all the shells off the floor, I don't want you to step on them and hurt your feet."

My mom sits near the stove, the warmest place in the house. We hear a car. We run to the window and see my dad getting out. A big man also steps out of the car and he's smiling. We run to open the door. My mom is crying and all we want to know is, "what's it like in jail? Did they make you break rocks?"

"Be quiet girls, let me tell your mother. The man who owns the turkeys found out I didn't have work and that's why I tried to steal one. I think he was sad to see you and the girls alone on

Thanksgiving Day, so he went to the
police and told them to let me go."

"Thank God and thank the man who got
you out of jail," says my mom.

Thanksgiving morning is here. We don't
have to go to school so we stay in bed because it's
warm under the covers. There's a loud knock on
the door. We hear my dad talking to a man. My
dad keeps saying "thank you, thank you."

I jump out of bed to see what's going on and
here's my dad holding this skinny, shabby
turkey. I look at it and the poor bird looks at me
and we both look surprised.

"Oh boy, go chop his head off Dad, so we
can cook it."

We sit down for our Thanksgiving Day
meal that consists of the same food we always eat.
Beans and tortillas, potatoes and tortillas, stew
and tortillas. The turkey is tied to a kitchen chair
with a string tied to his skinny leg. We throw bits
of tortilla and he pecks them off the floor.

We never ate that turkey. My dad built a
pen for him. We named him Roy, after Roy
Rogers, our favorite cowboy. Roy lived a happy
life. On cold nights my mom brought him into
the kitchen to keep warm.

Many years later Roy went to sleep on his favorite blanket and didn't wake up. We buried him in the back yard with a headstone on which is written:

HERE LIES ROY

THE BEST TURKEY

THE GARCIAS EVER HAD

The Coach

by Brian Silsbury

As a member of the Shanklin Sandown Rowing club in the 1950s, I cannot remember when Charlie, our coach, first appeared. We quickly learnt he was not a Chas, a Chuck, or even a Charles. He was Charlie and 'woe-be-tide' anyone deviating from that.

We had no idea how old he was. Suffice it to say, Charlie looked like the ancient mariner, craggy, weather-beaten with a face like a deeply wrinkled prune!

His joint passions were coaching oarsmen and swigging beer! He had set himself a goal of teaching us, a crew of pimply, callow youths, to be skilled oarsmen. Naturally, he hoped that one day, we'd win the South Coast Rowing Championships. To help achieve his goal, Charlie used extensive rowing knowledge and a wicked, caustic wit usually hurled from the coxswain's seat. Most summer evenings in the week, we'd practice racing starts, buoy turns and high stress finishes. But Sundays were different. Sundays were when Charlie arrived by bus from Ventnor and took charge.

Our purgatory would start as we launched the galley. Charlie would wade out with us having already grabbed the cox's seat. This meant that he was right in our faces, so we had nowhere to hide.

"In Bow and Two, out oars, move it, in Three and Four, take it away all," he barked as he nimbly slid aboard.

"OK, check that the oars are locked into the rollicks and your feet are firmly strapped into the stretcher."

Once underway, he was merciless. "Eyes in the boat Number Three," he yelled at me. "Bow, you're bloody breastfeeding that oar! Pull it into your guts, not your tits!" Charlie was in his element now.

Sometimes, he would become so passionate, that spittle and the white salt spray would congeal in the wrinkles each side of his mouth making him look like a mad dog! He always crouched at the back, poker faced and gimlet eyed. In rough seas, he invariably became blinded because his glasses were caked with salt from the flying spume. This happened when we drove the galley hard into the waves. It was uncanny, he could still detect when we were doing something wrong.

"You're digging too deep Number Three, square the blade before it enters the water or you'll catch a bloody crab!" he railed.

Afterwards we would congregate in the pub. By then Charlie had relaxed with a pint of bitter in one fist and a cigarette in the other. Leaning back expansively, he'd start. "Did I ever tell you about the time we launched the lifeboat in a force eight gale?"

"No Charlie," we chorused, desperate for him to change the subject from his vitriolic rowing critique.

"Yes, we went and rescued" ....and Coach Charlie was off, regaling us with one of his hoary seafaring tales again.

Who I Am

by Frank Warren

I am the sand hills of the Nebraska panhandle and the Platte river that flows below them.

I am Cheyenne, Wyoming where hail stones shattered milk bottles on our basement steps. Some cowboys, then, were a leavin' Cheyenne.

I am my father molding popcorn balls by kerosene lamp light for me and my twin brother Bill in our little company house at Rouse Colorado in 1928. I am the little pine tree just behind our outhouse blown to bits by a lightning bolt.

I am my parents packing our 1924 Essex car for a trip to California.

I am a tiny church on the hill above our once house. I am Rouse, now behind us. Roberta Hart, a little neighbor, promises to love and care for our big dog "Blackie." A photo, now beside me, shows girl and dog wearing big smiles.

I am Seligman, Arizona where we learn the "Mother Road," route 66, offers only dirt and gravel for the 450 miles to "Notre dame la Reina de Los Angeles and the Porciuncula River."

I am two tattered biplanes tied to a fence. Can't we find a way to take them with us? "Nope" is my father's response.

I am Compton, California and a family reunion. I am the big picnics held to welcome new arrivals from all over the 48 states. I am the forest of oil derricks on "Signal Hill." I am the strange smell of the place that upsets many but smells like money to others.

I am our move to San Luis Obispo where San Luis mountain and Bishop's Peak frame the view to the west. To the north, Cuesta Grade road was a traveler's nightmare.

I am my father, Roy, trying his best to get a motorcyclist and his son to a hospital. I am the long hours we sat in the too warm sunlight with our mother waiting Roy's return to us.

I am the dark pit of Junior High. I am the good teachers and a one act play wherein the prettiest girl in our class played the lead.

I am Senior High with better times. My brother and I illustrated the school newspaper and our class book. There was a girl who made me get to class early but I was too afraid and shy to ask for a date. Many years later at a class reunion, she said that she also hurried to see me in the same class room. She married a successful medical doctor who was also a successful novelist and a good guy.

I am all these episodes and as my High School French declares: "C'est la vie."

Compassion
by Joy Ehle

It's December 1997, and I'm visiting my son, Karl, in his new apartment. He's at work; so today, it's just the kitty and me. I'm curled up in the corner of a soft comfortable couch reading a book by my favorite author. On the opposite side of the room the kitty is fast asleep in her bed warmed by Colorado sunlight.

Kitty has a name and it's Dog; although, I prefer to call her Doggie. Nine years ago, a six-week old calico kitten was found wandering near campus in Houston by some students at Rice University. Somehow the tiny creature ended up in the dorm room of my son and his three roommates. They searched and advertised but had no luck finding her owner. Even though it

87

was against dorm rules they decided to risk keeping her. The chance that anyone would ever be able to spot a cat or any animal living in a boy's dorm room was extremely improbable.

The roommates pooled their money to have her spayed. She roamed the halls and memorized the girl's rooms where she was given milk and treats. One of the roommates had a girlfriend who was allergic to cats; so, it was only logical to call her Dog.

Doggie is affectionate toward Karl, but is conflicted about me. I live in Sedona, Arizona and she doesn't see me very often. Doggie allows me to pet her when I arrive for a visit -- but that's it. I've never owned a cat so I don't know much about them. Doggie apparently isn't aware, or just doesn't care, how much dogs like me. Personally I think it should count for something.

Perhaps Doggie is so touch-me-not-ish because somewhere on her travels something happened, trust became difficult for her and she developed a standoffish attitude. I can relate.

Whatever the reason, she's content now and skillful at keeping secrets.

I slowly turn the last page of the book I don't want to end. My eyes start to water. Books and movies rarely make me emotional but if the plot involves one soul touching another in a time of need -- well -- I cry like a baby. The daughter in the story has been searching for purpose and belonging and finally finds it in the home where she grew up. She will stay to help her ill father. I close the book and tears run down my face.

I wipe my eyes with the backs of my hands and glance up. To my surprise, Doggie is studying me. She slowly gets out of her bed, gingerly tiptoes toward me with her tail slightly raised. I remain completely still but cry a little more -- on purpose. Doggie jumps up on the couch, her eyes glued on me. When I pretend to cry again Doggie's little wild spirit reaches out to ease my pain. She climbs into my lap, lies down and starts to purr.

Saturday Night

by Barry Shulman

Saturday night
Neath State Street lights
Youthful breasts
And skirts too tight

Mothers and daughters
All look alike
In Chevrolets
Or on a bike

Inhibitions completely free
State's our own
Champs Elysees

Music echoes off the walls
Men succumb to siren calls
Like mariners in ancient seas
Seduced again

The View from Here

That wicked breeze

Sushi, ribs or bouillabaisse
Food from almost every place
Movies, concerts, jazz or blues
Folks off this week's Princess Cruise

Lost Atlantis, Camelot
The world has come to love this spot
Every language one can speak
Chinese, Russian, even Greek

Nikons, I phones everywhere
Not a worry, not a care

As State Street welcomes
Sunday's dawn
Last night's glitter
Now is gone

Designer benches occupied
Not by last night's pretty bride

Hunger now is everywhere
Last night's cupboards
Now are bare
Fighting off last night's cold
People young and people old
Homeless folks still have their rules
Each in search of last night's jewels

Each knows his place
And takes his turn
Things our neighbors had to learn

Too many homeless
Hungry too
Shelters for the lucky few

Enjoy our nights and all they bring
But keep in mind a simple thing
Not to share with those with less
And you might live at their address

Fortunado's Revenge

by Bill Livingstone

"I hastened to make an end to my labour. I forced the last stone into its position; I plastered it up. Against the new masonry I re-erected the old rampart of bones. For half of a century no mortal has disturbed them."

(The last sentences of <u>The Cask of Amontillado</u>, Edgar Allan Poe)

Now, in the 21st Century I am an old man, and the iron chain of conscience, guilt, and regret have drawn me back, to the bowels of my old palazzo, *Montresors*. Its imminent demolition and my memory of that day 50-years ago leave me powerless to resist – I must revisit the scene of my crime – that scene of my act of hate and revenge for his insult, an affront, otherwise, long lost in

95

the dust of time.

Deep in the ancient catacombs, insufferably cold and damp, for it lay below the bed of the River Arno, I shuffle forward; my flashlight pierces the darkness, my mind endeavors to pierce the fog of memory now fading. At the end of the deepest vault I perceived what must be the crypt where I took my revenge upon the drunken Fortunado on that festival night so many years before. The rampart of bones I placed before it have turned to dust and they no longer hide the obvious difference between the ancient granite walls and my shoddy attempt at masonry 50 years ago.

With the hammer and chisel, I chip away at the stones now firmly concreted in place -- each strike reechoes through the old catacomb where once only the sandaled footfalls of servants of Florentine nobility could be heard. When at last I have pierced my old friend's cell, I smell the dank putrid air of mildew -- it rushes over me like a wave of ghastly guilt.

But I must persevere, I must free my soul of this remorse; I am compelled to face Fortunado's remains. Only then can I end the haunting memory of my ancient crime. Each stone once so hastily mortared in place, I now laboriously remove and cast aside. When at last the aperture is large enough for me to enter Fortunado's cell, with flashlight in hand, I crawl through.

There, from the iron staples in the granite wall, hangs the rusted chain and padlock – Fortunado's final vestige. But where are the bones of my old friend? My torch scans the cell in vain. Where, in this putrid air are the conical hat, the jingling bells, and the tight-fitting party-striped costume? I find only a few ounces of moist dust on the damp earthen floor – the issue of a half century of mildew and rot.

While I ponder the void in my victim's tomb, I hear the shout of a distant voice. I cup my ear to hear the better, and I perceive the words shouted again, "Fire in the hole!" At first I'm puzzled by the words and hesitate.

A few moments later I hear a thunderous explosion and my mind instantly realizes the demolition of the old palazzo had begun -- a day earlier than I anticipated. But before I can turn to flee the cell, a great granite column falls across the opening and my fate is sealed; it is the fate of my victim, Fortunado.

A wrong is unredressed when retribution overtakes its redresser. (From <u>The Cask of Amontillado)</u>

Just

two seniors taking a morning walk

slower steps now ... eyes on ground

silver haired ... bodies gentled by time

    one ~ slight hitch in her right knee

    the other ~ stiff left leg

Just ...

    a stroll

noses alert ... sniffing the cool fall air

smelling damp leaves ... mudded dirt

beneath their feet

smiling at the crisp ... crackle ...

    ... crunch of liquid amber leaves

Just...

    enjoying the day

their health

bonded by years of love

Just…

two old broads

me and my dog

Beth Thompson

The Bad Day

by Robert A Reid

It didn't begin as a good day when he awakened at 4:00 am and couldn't get back to sleep. At breakfast he lost his cool when the wife berated him for not putting the toilet seat down and a few of his other failings. In response to his anger, she developed a sudden case of lockjaw and was unable to speak to him anymore that morning. There was an accident on the freeway and the usual stultifying 20-minute drive to work took over an hour and, of course, his reserved parking spot was taken by that new guy in sales that everybody disliked.

An advertising campaign presentation that he had worked on for three months and placed on his boss's desk yesterday had been thrown back on his desk labelled D.O.A. (Dead on Arrival) with a note scrawled on the cover, "you hopefully can do better than this." He needed a three

Martini lunch but at this company you'd get fired for that behavior so at noon he ordered take-out Chinese from the place around the corner and asked his suddenly surly secretary to pick it up for him. When she dropped the bag on his desk, he asked her to hold his calls and settled in for a much needed break. He opened the wire-handled box of bean sprouts, stuck in his chopsticks and out crawled a rather exotic looking worm. All this and it was only midday.

The afternoon dragged by and, while there were no severe setbacks, there was also no creativity. He simply couldn't work on the rejected presentation nor could he concentrate enough to begin a new one so he mostly leaned back in his chair and mused on his life and his lack of accomplishment. He wasn't particularly unhappy with his marriage. It had been seven years and the famous itch to try something new hadn't grabbed him and hopefully not her. His job was stable and they had enough money to live a solid upper middle-class life and raise their 3 year-old son. The early hour of awakening finally caught up to him and he fell asleep.

When he awoke, it was dark outside and he was disoriented. He looked at the clock in panic and saw it was only 5:30 pm, but it was November and the shortest day of the year loomed on the horizon. He stepped into the empty office and took the elevator down to the parking lot. What he really wanted was a drink but he knew that if he stopped at a bar now and came home late smelling of booze, the crime of toilet seat negligence would seem a misdemeanor compared with the grief that came from that transgression. So he got in the car and headed for home.

If he wasn't going to have a drink, then he needed a jolt of something to restore his usual enthusiasm and joy of life. He swung open the front door and it appeared in the form of his mop-headed three-year old boy who upon seeing his dad jumped up, threw his arms around his neck and hollered, "Daddy's home!"

Haiku
by Mary Frink

Magic on a wing

lucent, intoxicating

evanescent bird

When Will Mankind Ever Learn
by Barry Shulman

When will mankind ever learn
Bullets kill and missiles burn

We teach our children
Right from wrong
That wars are won
If you are strong

How many times will history teach
A world at peace is out of reach

Leaders of nations
Conjure fear
Warning their people
"The end is near"

To attack their neighbors
Before they defend

Do it now or "Our lives will end"
Every daughter, every son
Must learn to shoot the latest gun

Ships and planes
Are paramount
We must have more
Don't stop to count

Schools can wait
And elders too
These leaders don't seem
To have a clue

Think again before we sail
Guns and bullets always fail

To stay in power
Leaders preach
"Peace is now within our reach"

"War comes first

Just heed my call
Do not let our nation fall"

Wake up mankind
Go to school
The pen must be
The peoples' tool

Words not threats
Must now ring out
Do not whisper
We must shout

If we fail
To stop this madness
Our children's dowry
Will be sadness

The legacy we gift our young
A song of peace that was not sung

Summer Day

by Margaret Roff

Beautiful flowers on the UCSB Campus - pink, purple, yellow, red, orange and white.

Green grass despite the drought. The tiny yellow flowers are no longer here.

Birds chirping as they fly from bush to bush to tree.

The blue sky over the ocean; the puffy white clouds hovering over the mountains.

Another summer day along the south central coast of California.

Thank God for the Dog!!!!!

by Barbara Godley

Our one and only dog, Four-in-Hand Polka Dot, was six months old when I was four and she was the only dog I grew up with. She couldn't be a show dog because of her markings.   Most Dalmatians are light with dark spots and red rimmed eyes, but Polka Dot was much darker, with dark, "deer like" eyes. We all loved her and she knew it. She was queen of the neighborhood and we took her on all our hikes in the foothills as a protector against wild animals and snakes.

One summer, when I was ten, we went to the pear orchard for a week or two. My father was there all summer and we would play in the irrigation water, swim in the mucky reservoir, and play paper dolls with a neighbor girl. On the way home, mother noticed several large, round dark openings in the hills as we drove by. They'd been there for years, but for some reason, mother got interested in what they were and so we parked and walked quite a way up the hill to the openings. They were old abandoned mines left over possibly from the 1800s. We didn't have a flashlight, matches or anything to light the darkness, but we did, thank heaven, have our dog with us.

We walked through the opening into a pitch black walkway and slowly proceeded down the path. We couldn't see a thing and suddenly the dog screeched to a halt and mother tried to get her to keep going. "Go on Polka Dot, move!" But she wouldn't. Finally Mother picked up a stone and threw it and we heard it go whistling through the air and land in water way below.

Dogs must have wonderful instincts because our dog saved our lives. We left the mine, came down the hill, drove home and I have remembered this incident all my life.

Thank God for Polka Dot!

America's Forgotten Patients
by Sharon Alvarado

A scream, loud and piercing, bounced along the narrow hallway with the yellow stained walls. Another scream was followed by a sharp blow and a thump. I turn to see a skinny arm held in the grip of a large red hand. He is on the floor, legs folded toward his body. His head down. I can hear muffled cries as she strikes him. In her free hand she holds a wooden ruler, bringing it down repeatedly against his white pasty skin.

I look around, no one moves, nothing is said. I try to make eye contact with the nurse across from me. Her head down, she tugs at the corner of the bed; smoothing the sheet, pulling the blanket tightly against the thin mattress.

Is this happening? This is real. There are several nurses in the unit; they do not react to the cries of this very small boy.

What should I do? What am I doing here?

• • •

I was so excited my first day attending Fairview State Hospital in Costa Mesa, California, in 1963; I had been accepted into the Psychiatric Technician Program. I would attend school and work twenty hours a week at the hospital, while I prepared to take the exam for a California State License.

Fairview State Hospital opened January 5, 1959 and occupies 752 acres. With an initial bed capacity of 2,622, it can house 4,125 residents. It looks like a park and a college campus combined; it includes a swimming pool, auditorium, a small animal farm, a large library and a recreational campsite.

In 1908 there were approximately 24 hospitals, with a total of 2,561 beds, available for treating the mentally ill in the United States.

Archaic methods of treatment are now being replaced with new hospitals and new antipsychotic medications.

Harry Sullivan demonstrated the impact of

a therapeutic milieu. Sigmund Freud had published research on the treatment of the mind.

The philosophy of the hospital was, "All people have value as human beings. People do not lose their inherent value simply because of a disability."

It was the first day of school; dressed in white, my uniform rustled when I walked. A new beginning, my long-term goal: a Clinical Psychologist with expertise in Forensics.

Fairview was a new hospital with new ideas. Experiments were conducted in the effectiveness of LSD on severely emotionally disturbed children. Because of such a high population many experiments could occur simultaneously.

The hospital's mission statement focused on human dignity as well as education and research. Patients would be treated with compassion.

My drive into the facility was my journey into a new world. I felt like I was going to college. First, two weeks in class: orientation and instruction. The atmosphere was stimulating. Finding a seat, introductions, pulling out papers and pens and, as always, the sexual tension in a room full of young men and women. I was 21 years old. We were presented with the hierarchy of care doctors, nurses, psychiatric technicians and the entire ancillary staff it takes to manage thousands of patients. The facility had its own medical hospital; independent of the units housing the general population.

Some units had children as young as three years old. Many children were diagnosed with mental retardation, schizophrenia, autism and severe emotional disturbance. Children that were mentally competent, but who had such severe physical deformities that they were rejected by society and their families found a home in Fairview State Hospital. The morning went by quickly. I knew I was on the right road.

I had not read the Press-Telegram newspaper: June 8, 1963: "Five More Fired at State Hospital Fairview: Nine Total"

"Five more Psychiatric Technicians were fired from the staff at Fairview State Hospital in Costa Mesa after an investigation into brutality charges at the mental institution."

• • •

Two weeks of classroom instruction have passed, today we will go behind the beautiful park facing the public street. Classes are held in the Administration building, it sits gracefully amidst green grass and purple pansies. We had not wandered the grounds or entered any patient unit. Patient units are not open to the public and they are arranged in such a way that the enclosed day areas are not visible to visitors.

Mentally retarded patients were housed according to diagnosis, age and ability to ambulate.

The term "mentally retarded" is a diagnostic term; denoting categories of mental functioning such as "idiot", "imbecile" and "moron." These terms were derived from early IQ tests. The broader term "Developmental Disability" includes mental retardation, epilepsy, autism and cerebral palsy, as well as other disorders.

Non-ambulatory units included the profoundly mentally retarded; People with IQ below 20. They never left their unit and rarely left their bed.

Other units included patients with moderate to mild mental retardation and IQ between 35 and 69. Ambulatory and "trainable," these patients had privileges outside of their assigned units. Those with borderline intellectual functioning (IQ 70-84) were "educable" and were supposed to have different living units. I found they were frequently housed with the profoundly retarded for convenience or as "punishment." Behavior influenced housing. An attempt to keep the vulnerable patients safe resulted in isolating the severely violent patient. These units were referred to as the "80s": buildings 80, 81, 82 and 83.

Building 80 housed males. A cell designed for the "violent" patient had padded walls, no furniture, no windows, a small sink and toilet in one corner and a mattress on the floor. No one ever entered the room alone. A triple locked door had a small 4 by 8 inch window that you could look into and observe the patient. At meal times three orderlies would bring a paper tray of food with a plastic spoon. One would stand at the door, one carried and placed the food on the floor and one never took his eyes off the patient.

Five of us were touring this unit. We stopped at room 5. The Charge nurse explained that this patient had no mattress because he had destroyed two of them. These were not ordinary mattresses, but mattresses that were reinforced, specifically made to withstand any attempt to tear or destroy. This patient did not wear clothes. He would destroy and tear into bits any material item.

My turn at the window, I looked in. He stood to one side of the room: naked, tall, broad shoulders, tapering powerful legs, his head up, listening.

He was beautiful.

He was the most violent patient in Building 80.

This was the beginning of my real education. The reality of mental disorders. I would see physical beauty in the most depraved, I would be drawn to their perfection and to them. I would see gross ugliness in the innocent and avert my eyes.

The day would come when I would question my faith in God and turn away from all I had once believed.

•   •   •

We visited a sample unit in each area of treatment, ending with the children's section and the hospital. Next week working in the units would begin. Our visit to the units was our "orientation." Students were expected to do anything asked by the nurse in charge, equivalent to what many think of as a "nurse's aide." The Philosophy: actual work is the best teacher. Observation of licensed staff and classroom assignments would prepare us for taking the licensing exam after a year.

My first assignment was the non-ambulatory unit. It was arranged like an army barracks with long rows of beds against the two walls. The beds along one wall contained bars. They resembled cribs and small patients, not necessarily young, lived here. In the center of the room were two more rows of beds. Thus with two long walkways you could have four rows of ten beds, all butted up to each other. The head of one bed pushed against the tail of the next bed. A nurse's station was at the entrance of this unit.

At the rear of the unit was a bathroom for staff. Beyond that was the "tub" room. The walls and floor were tiled and there was a drain in the center of the room. There were six stainless steel pedestal tables, each with a built in sink. A lip approximately 3 inches high surrounded the table which also had a drain in the center. At one end there were several brushes with long handles and a high-pressure hose. This was the equipment used to clean these patients. There were no chairs at the bedsides. Visitors to this unit were rare.

Meals, brought from the main kitchen in carts, did not resemble food but rather bowls of green, brown and yellow paste. Spoons were supplied. The patients were spoon-fed this puree. More than once I heard the comment: "shovel the shit in, scrape the shit off. That's the job."

• • •

Having experienced most of the units now, ambulatory and non-ambulatory, high functioning and non-functioning, I realize there is a smell that will never leave these rooms. The wall, mattresses and floor have absorbed the odors of old food, all human fluids: blood, urine, mucous, semen, spit, vomit, sweat, menstrual blood flow, pus from open sores, unwashed bodies, bad breath from rotting gums and the stench of wet and dry feces.

What permeates into the very bones of those living and working in these conditions is more than the above. It is the desperation of despair. Palpable is the abandonment of hope and the wait for death.

I work in several more units. Every bodily

function of man and woman is revealed in nakedness. Every primitive urge known to man or woman is before your eyes.

A woman sits in the corner her shift pulled up; her hand inside her body. Spittle runs down her chin. Another sits in a corner sucking contently on her own breast, oblivious to all around her; in a room with eighty other patients, most profoundly retarded, some clearly psychotic, this behavior does not warrant a second glance.

I think I have seen it all and then I visit Unit E, a non-ambulatory unit.

My assignment is to do rounds. Moving between the beds I take a deep breath. I am trying to be cool, calm, professional and mature. I am none of these things. I am shocked by what I see and smell. I am not sure I will survive this rotation.

What is on her face?? Her hand is limp on her forehead. I move closer. Her body is twitching, she makes a gurgling sound.

Oh my God!   Oh my God!

I am running, help! HELP! I slip in feces and regain my balance.

Her eye….her eye….

Her eye is on her cheek. "Help…"

The two RNs in the nurse's station look at my face and start laughing.

"Calm down, calm down. She knows you're new. That's her way of welcoming you to the unit."

"What did you step in? It stinks, go clean your shoes."

"Aren't you going to do anything? Her eye is on her cheek."

"Yeah, we'll take care of it. One day we won't get it back in."

"That'll fix the little shit."

• • •

I have seen things that I will never forget. I do not know if I can describe it. Who will believe me? Can you see a half dozen patients climbing a chain link fence, clinging to it looking around without focus, one with spit drooling from the

126

corner of his mouth, white hospital pajamas loose, soiled?

So clearly animals in a cage. Dozens of "clients" milling around in this enclosure. The outdoor area sits in the back of the unit, there is a basketball hoop at one end, cement with a large drain in the center. No one is playing basketball. One or two sit on cement benches; most just wander, looking drunk, without purpose. Some squat and urinate; no one notices. At the end of the day it will all be washed down that drain.

How to describe the fear I felt when I walked into a unit with more than fifty people, the noise, a cacophony of sound. Alert to something new they turn your way, wanting to touch you, some eyes, reflecting maniacal intensity, others dull as though they see nothing.

Out of my mouth come the words: "HANDS DOWN," sounding louder and harsher than I intend, two words taught the first day of class. The dryness in my mouth and the clench of my stomach when a large woman reaches out and touches my hair. I am repulsed by some of them, I don't want them to touch me. Inside the day room, a woman on the floor masturbating. The laughter of the long experienced tech who sees my discomfort and makes a smart remark. There are too many people, all wandering without purpose, gross, human smells overwhelming. I cannot help these people. What help is there for them? I ask if I can fold the laundry and clean behind closed doors. The charge nurse assigns me tasks that take me off the floor.

• • •

After several months I do not have to make a decision to quit the program or resign from the hospital. I wake up one morning, my temperature 104.4 degrees. I am taken to the hospital where I will remain for two weeks. The first week I am in complete isolation.

The doctor asked if I have traveled "overseas?" When he learns I work at Fairview State Hospital, he states: "Fairview State hospital is worse than a third world country."

My recuperation will take weeks, maybe months, but he says, "you will soon be yourself."

I knew I would never "be myself." I did not think I would get the stench out of my nostrils, the fear out of my bones. My core beliefs about God, parents, caregivers, family, patients all changed.

I knew I lacked the empathy, compassion, patience and understanding to work with this kind of patient population. I learned about my need for boundaries and personal space.

I also learned to be very grateful and appreciate the few that are truly there because they care about these humans; see their humanity beneath the ugliness of their existence.

I judge less harshly those that question the purpose of maintaining life without quality or purpose.

Like a dye cast I am changed forever.

Plants and Pots

by Joan E. Jacobs

Penelope Pearl purchased pepper plants and purple petunias and potting soil and two new pots and on her back porch she put the two new pots that held the potting soil and purple petunias next to two old pots she planted with pepper plants all of which cost Penelope Pearl a pretty penny although she was hoping she could sell the pumpkins from her pumpkin patch to cover the price of the pepper plants and the purple petunias and the potting soil and the new pots but no one purchased the pumpkins and Penelope Pearl wound up in the poor house because she spent all her pesos on the pepper plants and the purple petunias and the potting soil and two new pots and it's oh so pitiful.

Plein-Air Painting

by Suzanne Yoast- Perko

It was a day I will never forget…Early one morning about twenty years ago I was meeting a group of artists. We'd been drawing and painting together on locations for several years. Living in Santa Barbara, California offered a variety of picturesque views. Occasionally we met in an area with palm trees and the ocean or perhaps facing the lovely Santa Barbara mountains. Sometimes we drove a few miles south to Carpinteria and enjoyed capturing a view of the bluffs overlooking the ocean.

This particular day we had chosen a spot up the coast, north of Santa Barbara called Ellwood Beach, at that time a lovely secluded area hidden from view by towering eucalyptus trees. Behind them was a sloping hillside covered with wildflowers, with a long winding path down toward the ocean. On the left, lining the path were more eucalyptus trees. What an inspiring view to attempt to capture on canvas!

Everyone wandered around and chose a view they found most inspiring. After assembling our easels, we placed our canvases on them. We then mixed our various paints onto our palettes. Each of us had high hopes of conveying the beauty and atmosphere of the sea. I chose a spot near the top of the pathway looking down toward the sparkling ocean. When my oil paints were mixed just right, I took a brush and put the beginning idea of my composition onto the canvas: eucalyptus trees, winding path, sky and ocean.

It's amazing when I'm painting; hours can fly by. I'm never aware of the time. I call it active meditation. Four hours passed and it was near the usual time of pack up and head home…for everyone but me. Oh well, I always ended up staying longer because I work slower than anyone else. I was used to it but it was somewhat disconcerting because we were occasionally in an area way off the beaten path. This day was no exception. Everyone folded up their equipment and carried it back to their cars along with an interesting painting to show for their time and effort. As the last person drove away, I thought, "Must be nice to work so fast."

A few hours flew by as I continued to work on my painting, looking toward the beach still trying to capture the meandering path with the exquisite eucalyptus trees and ocean below. Huh? That was interesting...it looked like a person way down by the beach heading up the path. We hadn't seen anyone while we were painting. I thought, "Oh well." I mixed more colors and kept painting, glancing occasionally toward the figure making its way up the path. I squinted my eyes but couldn't make out if it was a man or a woman. It looked like someone wearing only the bottom of a wetsuit. "Huh?" I wondered what happened to the board. If they were surfing they must have left it on the beach. Oh yes, I guess it is a man wearing the bottom of a black wetsuit.

Continuing to paint, I glanced back again..."Oh my God!" I thought. Were my eyes playing tricks on me? It was a man all right...a potbellied, middle-aged balding guy wearing nothing but a pair of women's black bikini underpants, a black garter belt and black nylons. I was freaked out! What should I do? I had all kinds of art equipment with me. I couldn't just grab my stuff and hurry away. I sat there frozen in place.

When he got closer to me, I stared straight ahead at my propped up painting and said in a real chipper voice, "Sure is a pretty day today!" He walked past shoeless, tramping on the rocky path in his bizarre outfit. Apparently he wasn't worried about ruining his fancy nylons with a run or a hole.

For sure that was a day I'll never forget... even though I've tried.

A Cloud Convention
by Barry Shulman

Storm clouds deciding
Which way to go
One says rain
The other snow

That mountain range
Off to the west
Not too far
But still a test

Further south
No hills to climb
A journey swift
No wasted time

Farms need the rain
If we go east
Let's give their fields

A welcome feast
Who decides which way we go
Who gets rain
Who gets snow

Who gets wet
Who stays dry
A cloud committee
In the sky

Could it be
We have no choice
Our journey lies
In other hands
Fertile fields
Or fallow lands

Who will be warm
Who will freeze
The choice not ours
Our friend
The breeze

On The Bus

by Bill Livingstone

The heavy breasted black woman leans forward and in a whisky voice asks, "Yall's wetbacks ain't cha?"

The thin dark-complected man in a battered straw hat and sweat stained shirt glances back, a quizzical look in his eyes, shakes his head, and looks forward again.

The woman sits back in her seat, heaves a sigh and mutters, "Make no differunts. We all in the same boat anyhow."

Across the aisle a slender blond teenage girl in a thin print dress overhears, but ignores the exchange. She has her own problems – pregnant, kicked out by her parents, down to her last five dollars, without hope, on her way to nowhere.

The great San Joaquin Valley slides by in slow motion under the hot summer sun. The white sound of the Greyhound's diesel engine blocks out thoughts of her bitter life. She gazes out the window at the long straight rows of cotton plants, mile after mile. No thoughts enter her mind – transfixed by the passing carpet – row after row after row -- regiments of green lines passing like the spokes on a great wagon wheel.

"Y'all lookin' a mite sad, chil'. Y'all runnin' away from somthin'?" the black woman growls, but with sympathy in her voice. The girl glances in her direction then quickly back out the window. "Y'all headin' fo' Modesto chil'?" Still no answer. She presses on, "Y'all hongry, chil'?"

Hunger is the least of her problems, but the girl instinctively turns her head and softly says, "Yes."

The black woman reaches into her satchel and says "Then, you eat this san'wich. It's good. It's col' cuts on nice white bread. Y'all'll like it."

The girl reaches out her slender arm, and with a wan smile says, "Thank you," takes the sandwich, and bites into it. The little Mexican man turns around when he smells the sharp scent of baloney and glances at the woman's satchel.

"Y'all hongry too, Mista?" He doesn't understand her words, but knows her meaning, and nods. The woman smiles and says "Here yar, fella. Y'all'll like cold cuts."

The Mexican man takes the sandwich, bobs his head, and says, "Gracias Senora." He turns forward, tears the sandwich in half, nudges his seat partner awake, and gives one half to him. They eat their gift quickly, as if they might never see food again. Together they turn and say, "Gracias Senora," to their benefactor.

Behind the woman sits an old man, thin, and wrinkled, with a white beard. He clears his throat to say something. The black woman looks back and says, somewhat surprised, "Don' tell me y'all hongry too? I got one san'wich lef – you wan it?"

The old man says, "No ma'am. Your generosity has quite satisfied my thirst for the milk of human kindness."

Puzzled by what she hears, the black woman takes the last sandwich out of her satchel and starts to eat it.

The Mexicans, the girl, the old man, and the black woman watch the red-ball sun end its day as it touches the flat western horizon, and hope, somehow, someday, all will end well with them too.

A True and Factual Accounting of Shopping With Auntie (Age 96 1/2)
by Joyce Metz

PRE-SHOPPING REMINDERS:
Take water pill
Take Darvocet
Take nap
Take walker

SHOPPING FOR ICED TEA GLASSES:
Too short
Too tall
Too light
Too heavy
Too narrow
Too wide

SHOPPING FOR THREAD:
Not cotton
Not Coats & Clark

Not white

Not right

SHOPPING FOR KITCHEN RUG:

Too blue

Too green

Too small

Too big

Too thin

Too thick

SHOPPING FOR SHELF PAPER:

Too wide

Too narrow

Too flowery

Too expensive

Not white

Not right

SHOPPING FOR A WEDDING CARD:

Too sweet

Too plain

Too large
Too small
Too cheap
Too much

RETURN HOME:
Kick off shoes
Hit the booze
One shot
Not quite
Two shots
Just right

Katmandu

by Gerson Kumin

When my father and I arrived at the airport at Katmandu, we were met by a couple by the name of Price. There was a brief pause while my father explained my presence. After we went through the Nepalese customs, the Prices, who had come in a jeep, drove us to what would be our home in Katmandu.

Our home in Katmandu had a name that when translated into English meant "a quiet corner". It was located off a side street away from the downtown area. Downtown consisted of a paved street leading from a Buddhist Temple, through the city, past numerous homes, shops, and offices, to another temple which looked like a pagoda. This was the home of Nepal's Kumari, a

147

young girl who was supposed to be a "living goddess". The street that we came down was the only paved street in the city. Most of the others were dirt roads along which cows that were sacred in the Hindu religion, wandered freely.

This street was also the parade route for the different religious festivals. During the festivals, music was played that was discordant to the Western ear. Thus it was good that we lived in "a quiet corner". I lost track of the numerous Hindu and Buddhist festivals. There was one where the Kumari was carried through the streets. At each festival people threw saffron colored rice, which went everywhere. If we were to watch from the sidewalks, we needed a shower and fresh clothes afterwards.

While our location was good, I found the lifestyle primitive. Our bathroom toilet was a hole in the floor down which buckets of water were poured. On either side of the hole were marks to show where to put our feet. One of our neighbors, a Danish anthropologist named

Jorganson, showed us how to make a "thunder box". A thunder box was simply a wooden box with a hole cut in the bottom. This was placed over the hole in the floor. We used this when we needed to sit.

We had cold water in the house, both in the shower and the sink. In order to drink water, we had to boil it first. In the kitchen we had a tiny refrigerator and a Primus stove that used gasoline. The gasoline had to be pumped to pressurize it to produce a vapor which we lit for cooking.

Once Mrs. Price learned that I had come east to go to school, she mentioned that there was a school run by American Jesuit fathers just north of the city. The Godaveri School was 10 miles north of Katmandu. The Prices drove my father and me out there and, after a short introduction, I was accepted into the school. It was housed in what had been an old estate.

My new classmates were from the upper classes of Nepal. Our curriculum was taught in

English. The fathers were using a course from Cambridge University in England. It had been developed by the British when they occupied India.

In athletics I was introduced to two sports that were new to me; volleyball and football. I later learned that the football we were playing was called soccer in the United States.

We had a heavy load as far as classwork was concerned. In the sciences we were required to take all three sciences, Physics, Chemistry and Biology in the same year. In Geography we studied Africa as it was in 1958. Many of the countries that we studied have been renamed or become independent since then.

Again, I didn't like the sanitary facilities. The toilets were the typical hole in the ground. I found squatting for long periods difficult. At Godaveri at least we had showers. The problem was that they were cold showers. At one point I ran back to Katmandu in protest. After Dad poured hot water on me, I felt in good enough shape to face school again.

In 1958, after one year, Dad and I left Nepal. When I returned to Baltimore, I entered high school in the 11th grade. I have to give a great deal of credit to the Godaveri School. With its compressed classwork, it enabled me to jump from the eighth grade to the eleventh.

Life's Newest Game
by Barry Shulman

Welcome to life's newest game
Vanity is its name

Heredity was once a jewel
Your mother's eyes
Your father's hair
Were something you were proud to bear

Now the rules are upside down
You cannot make that trip to town
Not before you're mirror-round

As you walk through that door
Heading for the nearest store
Make a list and check it twice
Get your partner's best advice

Check yourself from top to bottom
Matching colors since it's autumn
Style is the theme this year
Sporting this month's latest gear

Height and weight are paramount
Pounds are something you must count

Though all these things are superficial
The rules they say are now official

All that makes us who we are
Is now inside a makeup jar

If vanity and looks prevail
Then all that counts is now for sale

All family values handed down
May never make that trip to town

The F. L. K.

by Robert A Reid

In an Obstetrical training program the experience is mostly one of volume. Oh sure, at a big inner city hospital there is plenty of pathology because of poor nutrition, educational lack and general poverty but despite these disadvantages pregnant women mostly try to take good care of themselves and their unborn children. For the resident on O.B., shifts of sleepless nights and somnambulant days are common. I was sleepwalking my morning rounds one day when a very alert student nurse approached.

"Hi, Doctor Kildare, my name's Carla. Did you notice that smallish baby you delivered at 3 this morning?"

"There were 13 overnight, they all looked fine to me," he responded.

"Well this one looked strange to me. His

nose has no bridge and he has a bumpy rash on his hands and feet. I looked it up and I think he may have congenital syphilis."

"My God! In all my training I've never seen a case. Let's go have a look."

Mother was rooming-in with the baby and when the pair arrived she was nursing. The infant seemed very content and was certainly sucking vigorously. From the side of his face it was obvious that he had a funny-looking nose which might be consistent with the "saddle nose" of congenital syphilis. Kildare reviewed the medical record and saw that the mother's syphilis test, the VDRL was negative but that test is done in early pregnancy and perhaps she contacted the disease later. All newborns are also tested but the results were not in yet.

"Is there a problem?" the mother asked.

"No, we just wanted to do a quick examination of your baby, if you don't mind."

"Not at all," she responded and handed the tiny bundle over.

The doctor laid the baby in the bassinet and unwrapped the blankets. The face was definitely weird with what could be described as a saddle nose but basically, unlike most babies, the kid was ugly. He did have some papules on the hands and the soles of his feet but they didn't look infectious. He rewrapped the boy and returned him to mom. Once outside of the room, the nurse asked, "What did you think?"

"First, Carla, let me compliment you on your good observation and investigation. At birth last night I didn't notice that the baby was unusual. I don't know whether he has congenital syphilis or not but at the least he is a F.L.K."

The nurse was puzzled. "What's a F.L.K.?

"Funny Looking Kid. Tell you what. I'll go down to the lab and check on the baby's VDRL and talk to you later. Thanks again for calling my attention to this."

While Kildare was consulting with the lab people and finding, to his relief, that the test was negative he received a call from Nurse Carla.

"How's the lab work?"

"Negative, thank God."

"I'm not surprised," she said. "Come on up to the unit. I think we have an explanation for everything."

Kildare raced up the stairs and went into the Post-Partum unit where a very unusual looking but proud father was holding the F.L.K. who was his spitting image.

In Front of Her

by Mary Frink

It's her last night in Cabo and she dines at the Agave at the resort. Her waiter also waited on her at the pool that day. Luis. He was quick and attentive, especially with unasked for Margaritas. Upon ordering, not seeing it on the menu, she wonders aloud if they have ice cream. Luis is already gone.

At the next table is a Trey Gowdy "look alike" wearing bright white flip flops she thinks Trey would never wear. But the thin face is similar and the hair is the same, one of the brilliant blonde iterations that Trey truly wore; one of many bad styles. The styled high platinum hair looks good on this man, with his white linen slacks and white linen shirt that is flicked with

159

small splashes of different brightly colored paint, like an artist had been wearing it all day to work in. But who knows, she muses, maybe she is wrong, maybe Trey <u>would</u> sport the flip flops.

She enjoys her chicken taquitos, which, along with another Margarita, and while remaining unseen, Luis has magically placed on her table. Upon thinking this, she notices a small boy, intent on drawing, sitting by the faux Trey. As she is gazing at him, secure in her invisibility of being an aged woman, he surprises her. He gets up and walks over and introduces himself. Faux Trey says, "I hope it's alright with you. We're trying to teach him to engage."

"But of course", she answers. She turns back to her place and there is a white oval dish of vanilla ice cream drizzled with chocolate sauce.

Two unexpected occurrences in the space of a moment. Perfect.

The Pantsuit
by Joy Ehle

It's 1999 and I'm driving north from Tucson in my little green Subaru as my friend, Barbara, drives south from Sedona. We plan to meet in Phoenix.

A friendship is like a favorite outfit: exciting when first found and more comfortable as time goes on. Barbara is the classiest of outfits: a Giorgio Armani with a soft Kentucky accent.

We have a common interest: basketball. Especially, Arizona Wildcat basketball. It was at one of our wine, popcorn and basketball parties -- when I lived in Sedona -- that we discussed the places in the world where we would like to visit. Simultaneously, we both said, "Machu Picchu."

I said something noncommittal like -- well - let's plan to take the trip someday. Barbara replied, "If we are going, we better do it now. I'm 75. It can't be an easy trip." Wow, I thought. She's serious. Is it possible I will actually travel deep into that remote part of Peru? Maybe some fantasies are possible -- after all.

I remember, as a child, studying a magazine full of glossy colored pictures of mysterious, orchid covered ruins that hugged rocky heights over vertical cliffs. What would it be like, I wondered and dreamed, to walk among the Inca spirits?

Barbara and I discussed over the phone and exchanged many emails about the clothes to bring on this trip. I described my perfect travel outfit from Dillards Department Store: a gray, 100% cotton, Liz Claiborne pantsuit with white trim, elastic waistband and pullover hooded jacket with a short zipper at the neck.

We snap each other's photo at Phoenix International Airport and then brace ourselves for bad news spewing from loudspeakers. Our flight is delayed. It's doubtful we will make the connection in Dallas. The Overseas Adventure Travel (OAT) tour is scheduled to depart from Miami on a 7:00 PM flight to Lima, Peru and we won't be with them.

We arrive in Miami at midnight to a deserted airport. The good news: American Airlines will treat us to a room in the airport hotel. The bad news: they lost our luggage but assure us it will be on the next plane. The room at the hotel is quite nice, but chilly. Since I didn't bring any change of clothes (Oops) I keep my pantsuit outfit on for the night.

Barbara and I, in my gray Liz Claiborne suit, wander around the airport all day. We kill time by sampling food at restaurants and browsing shops until the 7:00 PM flight. At midnight, we arrive in Lima where we are confronted with a lot of instructions in Spanish by customs agents. The only person in the airport, who speaks a little English, is the baggage clerk. I think he's telling us that our luggage hasn't arrived with the plane.

I glance past a soldier holding an Uzi -- bandolier bullet belts crisscrossed across his chest -- to throngs of yelling men outside. I tell this sort-of English speaking person that there's no way we are going out there. A representative from OAT is supposed to meet us but now, to our dismay, we learn no visitors are allowed into the airport. The baggage clerk finds someone -- I was hoping for a bigger man -- to guide us through the crowd to a person holding a tiny cardboard OAT sign.

Barbara and I slip into the back seat. The driver doesn't speak English and the person who carried the sign, only barely. If I look at Barbara she will know my fear. We sit close together but don't speak. Is she as scared as I am? Will our families ever hear from us again? Our hometown newspapers will probably run a small article saying we were last seen at the Lima airport before we disappeared.

Even though I'm tired my eyes are wide open. Buildings flash by the car windows. Armed guards are stationed in front of all large homes. Finally, we stop at a modest hotel, climb up cement steps and wake up the owner. My Liz pantsuit is asked to serve double duty as pajamas again tonight. Dark brown water flows out of the faucets so taking a shower tomorrow morning is out of the question.

We arrive at the airport for an early flight to Cuzco and the baggage handler greets us with a big smile. Our luggage has caught up with us. A member of OAT meets us in Cuzco and drives us to a place in the Urubamba Valley where our fellow tour members are enjoying a picnic and float trip in inflatable rafts. I pass on the invitation and wave to Barbara as she disappears down the river. I can only ask my pantsuit to do so much.

It's late when we arrive at Posada del Inca Hotel in Yucay, Peru. I drop onto a bed -- exhausted. Barbara glances toward me. "You know you still look pretty good. Where did you say you bought that pantsuit? I'd like to buy one too."

This story is dedicated to the memory of my dear friend, Barbara Fisher.

Distraction
by Douglas Huston

Crows, loud in the forest

chasing away a predator

and my wondering thoughts

A call from another city

with the sound of a friend's laughter

Two puppies wrestling

focused on each other

entertaining me alone

A warm gentle breeze

across my face

telling me I am

where I need to be

I As He/She

by Joan E. Jacobs

Do I write as she though I'm I? Do I write as I and pretend I'm she? Am I third person or second person? Do I write as he and pretend I'm she? Or do I write as third person and pretend I'm she? Perhaps I'm to write as second person and pretend I'm he.

What about an it? Do I write as it and pretend I'm I? Or do I write as she and pretend I'm it?

How about writing as you? Do I then write as you and pretend I'm he or even I? Or am I whosit and writing about whatsit?

Confused? You should be in my shoes trying to figure out if my voice is to be I, she, he, it, you, whosit, second person, third person, singular or plural, subjective or objective.

Broken Bread
by Barry Shulman

I've broken bread
With royalty

And blessed the dead
On bended knee

I've kissed the breasts
That all have sought

And drunk the wines
The vines have brought

Wild rivers, mountain tops
Lightening, thunder
Soft rain drops

Every culture, every food
Laughter, silence

Every mood

Tchaikovsky, Chopin
Or Les Mis'
A foreign film or Ramos Fizz

Memories of distant lands
Are now lost in shifting sands

A ship at sea
Without a keel
Emotions I could never see

Life's game played out
Much too fast

The present now
Has killed the past

China

by Anna Anderson

Hello! I'm Mrs. Herr's mother-in-law. Mrs. Herr's husband, Kevin, is my son. I'm Chinese. My mother and father are from Southern China.

China is one of the oldest countries around. One of the oldest human fossils ever found is "Peking Man" and he is about a million years old. Japanese, Koreans, other Asians and even the first hunters and gatherers that came to the Northern American Continent came from China.

China is known for starting the drinking of tea. There is an expression, "I wouldn't trade it or do it for all the tea in China." Some 3000 years before Christ was born, Emperor Shen Nuing's servants were boiling water on an open fire under a tree and some leaves fell in and made the water more pleasant to drink. Tea was discovered! It spread to other Asian groups and then to Europe until, in 1600, it became the national drink of Great Britain. They in turn sent tea to their American colonies. But they added a tax that the colonists didn't like so they dumped the tea into the ocean (this was known as the Boston Tea Party). This started the Revolutionary War in which the American colonies broke away from Great Britain.

Tea ceremonies still hold a place in English and Asian countries. Whether you go to a home or a restaurant, tea is a gesture of hospitality. In primitive societies, where they use rivers and streams to wash, bathe, and to do a few other things, water is not safe to drink. You don't offer a drink of water, you offer tea. In China, tea is offered to the eldest first because age is honored. Everybody in the family has his place. The mother, the father, the children, the aunts and uncles, cousins, members of the clan.

In China, around 3000 years B.C., Emperor Huang Ti had a mulberry tree that was droopy and asked his wife Si Ling Shi to find out what the problem was. She found big white worms were eating the mulberry leaves and spinning shiny cocoons. She accidentally dropped the cocoon in hot water and a delicate, cobwebby tangle separated itself from the cocoon. Si Ling Shi drew it out and found that one slender thread was unwinding itself from the cocoon. She had discovered silk. I understand that you have a mulberry tree in your backyard here. For 3000 years, Chinese made silk and sent it all over the world via the "silk route." Then the Roman Emperor Justinian objected to paying the high price of silk. First he tried to establish his own route to eliminate the Persians (now Iranians) from taking their cut. Then he sent two monks as spies and they sneaked out some silkworm eggs and some mulberry seeds in a bamboo cane. Thus, the Romans could make their own silk.

In addition to tea and silk, the Chinese invented printing, noodles, (Marco Polo brought noodles to Italy, creating spaghetti. Today it's called pasta!) gunpowder, and ice cream. They make fine porcelain, paintings, and carvings.

The Chinese have a rich cultural past, but today their biggest gift to the United States is their market potential. They have a population of a billion people, equal to four times our population. They need our goods: food, farm equipment, radios, televisions, washing machines, lamps, plumbing, utensils, etc. They need our technology: how to produce more food, crop rotation, fertilization, chemicals, pharmaceuticals, medicine, law, computers, communication, transportation, construction and financing. Hopefully we will be able to establish a good partnership for the good of both countries.

White Tennis Shoes
by Barry Shulman

White tennis shoes
That help my back
The ones I found on
Last year's rack

The price was right
The scuffs were slight
I think I'll try them out tonight

I've had good shoes
When times were better
Then I was young
A true jet-setter

The only problem
With those shoes
They hurt my feet
And left a bruise

But when I wore them
Out one night
My family said
The look was right

Too bad folks
This time you lose
I'm going to stick
With last year's shoes

The Promise
by Raven Wolfe

"Please come to the Christmas party. You never show up at any of our staff events."

"You know how I feel about socializing with work people. It's just not my thing."

"Of course. I understand, but still, I would love for you to come. It's really not that bad. You might even enjoy it." I find that last statement very doubtful. "Plus, you can bring a date." A date? Really? If I bring a girlfriend they'll all think I'm gay. Like I give a shit what they think? But still….

My roommate Russ agrees to come with me. He even agrees to wear something nice, unlike his usual huge black tee shirts and baggy pants and rubber thongs. He searches through the junk on his closet floor and comes up with a pair of fairly clean sneakers with matching shoe laces.

"Russ, I know this is a huge sacrifice. I really appreciate it. I owe you a big one." He nods his head and smiles. "Just don't embarrass me," I tell him.

"But embarrassing you is one of my favorite activities. I don't know if I can do that."

"Well, just try. OK?" Russ makes no indication that he will try. He knows everything about my personal life. He started out as a renter and now 5 years later, he is my best friend in the world. Russ sees me at my worst. We have the good sense to not have a sexual relationship, but on every other level, there is an ocean of psychological and emotional intimacy in our friendship. He can walk in the house, take one look at me and just knows what to say.

"What? He didn't call?" or "Shitty day at work?" or "Oops, I can tell you're premenstrual. I will keep my distance."

Four days later......

After three attempts at parallel parking, Russ manages to inch his way into the tiniest of parking spaces. Just a few blocks from the club where the dreaded staff party is being held. I take a deep breath. "Russ, I have a favor to ask." He looks at me with a suspicious smile. "Don't say no until you think about it for a few seconds. OK?" He nods his head. "OK. Well, you know how I generally can't stand socializing with people I work with?" Russ nods his head and lights a cigarette. "I know this may sound crazy. But I just want you to think about it." Russ takes five big puffs and throws the butt out of the car window. "Can you act like we are a couple? Like you are really in love with me?" He says nothing. "It's just that the other teachers already think I'm weird and if we can act like a couple, maybe they will, maybe, think I'm normal. Or something."

"You're kidding me. Right? This is a joke."

"No, I am serious."

"Are you fucking kidding me?"

"No, Russ. I'm not kidding. In all the years

I've taught at this school, I have never attended any kind of social function with the staff." Then I tell him that I would do the same for him. If he ever asked.

"Let me get this straight. You want me to act like I'm in love with you. Like your lover or something?" I nod my head yes. He takes a deep breath and says he will do his best.

At the party Russ behaves pretty much the way I want him to. He periodically puts his arm around me. He quietly asks me how I'm doing. We eat off each other's plates, like we do when we eat together at home. He's charming. For the most part, except when his eyes wander to the dance floor where very young and sexy women are dancing. That is when I have to kick him under the table. My colleagues seem to like Russ. He is very funny and can talk about anything. Occasionally someone will ask how we met and Russ, who is a screen writer, makes up different stories about our alleged relationship, the trips we never took, the romantic habits we don't have.

The precious little sayings we never say to each other. I just sit there and smile.

We stay as long as I can bear it. Eventually, I make my excuses and Russ and I are able to slip out of the restaurant and head home. As he pulls onto the freeway, I can feel myself relaxing. Breathing more deeply.

"Thanks, Russ. You were great. I really appreciate what you did."

"Really? Did you feel adored? Did I do a good job?"

"Oh yeah. You did a great job."

"You sure?"

"Oh yeah. You were fantastic. I hope no one asks me for more details of our so-called travels through Tunisia. I'm not even sure where it is." I go on and on, making sure he knows how very appreciative I am that we were able to pull it all off.

Russ explains exactly where Tunisia is on the map and then reminds me that I now owe him a big favor. "'I know, Russ. I owe you a really huge one." I have no idea what exactly that huge favor could be. He helped me paint my bedroom for my last birthday. It was the first time I ever saw someone paint inside a closet with all the clothes still hanging.

"Yep, you owe me a huge one." I reply that I will never forget.

Several months after the staff party, after being a renter in my house for a year, Russ takes advantage of an opportunity to move out. I have my doubts he will still want to remain best friends, but he insists that will never happen. To my surprise, the friendship remains just as close and caring as it has ever been. His new place is beautiful, up in the mountains with amazing views of the back country. We still share meals, go to movies, hang out together. I give him some furniture I no longer need, lots of kitchen supplies, cleaning supplies, a few lamps and new bed linen. Our birthdays are just a few days apart. He takes me out for a fancy meal for my birthday and for his birthday, he asks me to clean his bathroom. It is a pretty yucky job, but I am willing to do it. The day I come to clean, he is away at work and the job doesn't take as long as I had expected.

I have a brilliant idea. I will surprise him by cleaning his bedroom. I change his sheets, vacuum, polish the mirror, hang his clothes neatly in his closet, fold and put away all his clean laundry, dust and remove the paper he has used to cover the only window in the room. By the time I am done in his room, the room has changed from dark, dank, dusty and stinky, into a sunny and clean space with matching bed linens and fresh air from a now opened window. He, of course, loves all the work I have done and thanks me profusely.

"Now, if you meet someone special, you can bring her home to spend the night," I tell him. He looks doubtful. He claims that it will most likely never happen, but I encourage him to have some hope. I know him well. He has a low opinion of himself.

About a week later Russ calls and leaves a message on my answering machine. He claims he has "something amazing" to tell me. When I return his call, he tells me, excitedly, that he has actually met a woman who he actually likes, who actually spent the night at his place. Actually! And he likes her. A lot. I ask him what she thought of his bedroom. He claims that she loved how clean it was and she even complimented him on the cleanliness of his bathroom. For me, this is all I have ever wanted for Russ. He has been a loyal and loving friend, always there for me. Of all the gifts I have given to my friends, I think this is my favorite. I kept my promise. I returned his favor. And when I look back at all the men I have had in my life, Russ is the one who showed me that there are men with integrity and trustworthiness.

Thanks, Russ.

It Wasn't The Fruitcake

by Joyce Metz

After I moved to Valle Verde I started to receive Christmas fruitcakes from my brother, Dave. He always sent a Yahoo fruitcake. Just the name turned me off. When I wrote to thank him, I would add a little reminder of how every afternoon Moma and I used to enjoy a thin slice of Collin Street fruitcake and a cup of coffee. Oh, how good that was. Dave never took the hint. I continue .... for twelve years now, to receive Yahoo fruitcakes.

This year when my daughter, Holly, asked what I wanted for Christmas I whipped out the Collin Street brochure. "Here, this is what I want."

"But, Mom, it's only fruitcake. You could order it for yourself."

"No, I won't spend $50.00 on myself. For years I've thought about ordering it, but have never followed through. I keep getting those darn Yahoo fruitcakes from Dave, but it's Collin Street I want. That's what Moma and I used to enjoy. I'd go over to her house every afternoon. We'd sit in the kitchen and make a ritual of slicing the cake so thin you could almost see through it. That and a cup of International coffee and some good conversation about the day's events made for a very pleasant interlude."

This year when Christmas came I received the usual Yahoo fruitcake from Dave, but also the Collin Street fruitcake from Holly. I opened the Collin Street first, oh so good... what wonderful memories it stirred of happy afternoons shared with Moma. Then I tried the Yahoo. My eyebrows lifted in surprise. There was no discernible difference in the two fruitcakes. How could this be? I read the lengthy list of ingredients on each wrapping. The same, exactly the same. It took me all these years to realize what made Collin Street fruitcake so special wasn't the cake, it was Moma.

My Dad
by Sharon Alvarado

There was this time

This one time

We went fishing off the wharf

It was evening, not very many people

Mist settled over the ocean

Gray and still

We walked along the wharf; at the end there were
logs a few feet from the edge.

No guard rails; if you wanted to you could walk
right off the edge

I wasn't afraid

Men were fishing

There were buckets, you could see fish in them

Silver sliding in the water

The smell of brine in the air

Most people had a fishing pole.

We had a "drop line"

It had a "sinker" that would take it down into the water

My brother kept looking in the buckets, asking questions

He talked too much

My dad stood back

He took a cigarette from the pack

Camels, always in his shirt pocket

He lit the cigarette with a silver lighter

Making a sharp sound when he closed the lid

Standing back smoking his cigarette.

The smoke curled away from his mouth and

mingled with the mist

He was quiet

His shoulders rested

I watched him as he squatted down talking to a man.

He laughed

A quiet sound

The air easy around him

Gentle

There was this time

This one time

Adventures in Alaska

by John Ackerman

As a child, my father shared experiences about his participation in World War I. He was romantically attracted at age 17 visualizing himself to be a Captain on a gorgeous white steed. In fact, he was required to enter the Austrian/Hungarian army commanding 250 men in the trenches. His tales of the horror of cannon balls lopping off the heads of his soldiers were permanently and indelibly inscribed in my memory.

Subsequently, during the Vietnam War, having finally completed my formal medical education (including my "straight" internal medicine internship and psychiatry residency), I was then required as a U.S. male citizen to fulfill my military obligation. However, I had no interest in being involved in the war, so I discussed my options with my local Draft Board.

They advised me to contact the United States Public Health Service (USPHS) in Washington, D.C, They suggested that I visit Indian Reservations in Arizona, South Dakota, and Alaska and provided my wife and me with airline tickets to check all 3 possibilities. We chose Alaska. I received the rank of Lieutenant Commander overseeing all mental health issues of the 7 rural small hospitals in the Alaskan bush. USPHS moved our belongings and the adventure began.

There was in 1968, plenty of evidence of the major earthquake that shook the Anchorage area several years before. I was to be the only Indian Health Service psychiatric physician for the entire State working in the bush. I met the other two team members, one Ph.D. psychologist and one MSW psychiatric social worker. Each of the seven small bush hospitals was surrounded by dozens of Eskimo or Indian villages   We split up servicing those hospitals except, as the leader, I also had the final general responsibility for all.

Occasionally, away from the small hospitals, I dealt with unanticipated situations by phone or even face to face sometimes requiring a translator from nearby Russia. Keep in mind that the size of Alaska is equivalent to the entire USA.

Each small village communicated by short wave (twice a day) by a villager trained to do such work. If a patient did not improve, he or she would be sent to the nearest bush hospital. If clinical progression continued to be insufficient, the patient would be transported by a small bush plane to the large hospital in Anchorage.

On my_first day I found stacks of clinical files and bills piled up on my desk. Each file required my signature in order to release Federal monies to pay for the variety of medical and transportation bills. All such expenses would need to be covered by my annual budget of $125,000. As I placed my signature on each bill, anxiety mounted regarding the consequences should I make a financial mistake.

Before coming to Alaska, my wife, Ruth and

I were learning (in the "lower states") to prepare with the Lamaze birthing technique for the arrival of our first child. However, the Alaskan gynecologist knew nothing about Lamaze and proceeded with his usual approach. Thus Ruth's first birth took place in the large Anchorage Native Health hospital along with Eskimo and "south-east" native women.

While Ruth enjoyed our newborn son, I was flying everywhere throughout Alaska and the lower states (including Washington, D.C. and other large   cities) dealing with my responsibilities.

At one time, Ruth reluctantly agreed to go with me to the Tic Chic Mountains near Dillingham to fish in one of the mountain lakes. She hated the idea of fishing and brought a favorite book. At last, with much ambivalence, she finally cast her bait. Instantly, BAM!! It was a gorgeous 24 inch rainbow. Each subsequent 8 casts produced the same. She absolutely could not contain herself!!

One day's objective was to collaborate with child psychiatrist, Elinore Harvey, M.D. at the male Boarding school for Native Teenagers run by the Bureau of Indian Affairs (BIA) on the island of Sitka. We missed our commercial connection and needed to hire a small one-engine plane. As we plowed west over the ocean toward Sitka, the winds tossed us hither and yon as if we were mere feathers. We never thought we would arrive safely on the island's airport landing strip.

The urgency about getting to Sitka was due to an "epidemic" of suicides that had already taken the lives of 13 students. We met with the students and faculty and staff. We made many subsequent telephone consultations and were relieved that the "epidemic" was successfully stopped.

Dr. Harvey and I attempted to initiate a discussion with the BIA regarding the possibility of a trial school actually located in a village. Perhaps the Bureau of Indian Affairs might consider such a possibility? Students needed to be able to have regular contacts with family and friends in their own villages.

Prior to leaving Alaska, I spoke with the U.S. military base suggesting that they consider discussions with USPHS and the BIA regarding upgraded support for the benefit of the teenagers and their families living in Alaska. At the time they did not seem interested? In mid-1970 nearing the end of my service, the administrative center for the State of Alaska in Juneau contacted me to consider taking the position of Director of the Department of Mental Health. I thanked them for the opportunity, but declined.

Many years later, my wife Ruth and I took our children to Juneau. In order to land at the airport the jet had to dip under the cloud cover and, hugging the mountains on the right, sharply descend to the runway. Ruth, was so shaken by the maneuver that she insisted on staying at a bar while the rest of the family transferred to a helicopter with the intention of flying to the origins of several glaciers. On that flight, somehow, our eagle-eyed pilot spotted in the distance a mountain elk and flew us within 3-4 feet of that gorgeous specimen which in all of its glory remained completely unfazed. We then banked sharply to the left and flew over a series of mountains and valleys finally landing on the origins of the multiple glaciers. We deplaned onto the ice which was dotted with immense crevices that could gulp anything they wished. We walked around as if we were at the origins of human life. On our return to the airport and describing it all to Ruth, she confessed that she was very glad to have missed that experience.

When I look back over our years in our glorious largest state, I realize that the clinical work was very rewarding but my greatest gain in knowledge was in administration and finance that has served me well through the subsequent years. My fondest memory, however, other than the birth of our first child, is that magical day in the Tic Chic Mountains when Ruth caught all those beautiful Rainbow Trout and never looked at that book she had planned to read while I fished.

The Hit Man
by Robert A Reid

On a dark, moonless night a black stretch Cadillac pulled into the fog-shrouded circle of light cast by a street lamp. A burly man in a dark overcoat with his hat pulled low on his forehead stepped out of the passenger side and leaned back into the open window. The bulge under his left arm was apparent despite the thick garments.

"I don't know when these gamblers will get the message. You're not going to win and if you don't pay off your markers you will end up like that poor bastard tonight."

"Yeah, it's an old story but these suckers non capisce" came the reply from the driver.

"I'm kinda shocked that the boss would loan any money to a loser like this guy. Even at 10%

interest per week, there was no way in hell to ever collect and he was going to have to call on his soldiers to make an example of him. And so we did."

"Yeah, he must not have known who he was dealing with. The look on his face when he realized we were going kill him was haunting."

"You're new and mostly drive. After a while killing becomes routine and you get all kinds of looks before the bullet goes in. I gotta say that the most common is disbelief. They've seen this stuff in the movies but never believed it could happen to them."

The driver seemed to contemplate that last statement for a while. "Don't you feel any regret over snuffing some poor jerk whose worst crime is not paying his debts?"

"No, its only business. In the early days I even got a small thrill from the power I had but even that is gone now. It's just another day at the office and the pay is excellent."

"Maybe someday I'll get there too. I gotta go,

see you tomorrow." He put the Cadillac in gear and disappeared into the blackness.

The burly man straightened up, tightened his overcoat collar against the cold and strode to a nearby front door. He tried the latch but finding it locked, rang the bell. After a minute or two the door swung open and a diminutive figure framed in the interior light, cried, "Daddy, you're home!"

Where I'm From
by Joyce Metz

I am from outer space and so are you, but you
don't know it yet.
I know the moon and the sun and all the planets.
I am from bright, sunny skies.
From the star dust.
And from the debris we humans have left behind.
I am from a self-made entrepreneur and the
Earth's best mother.
From Butch and Florence and brothers, Don and
Dave.
I am from liberal thinkers and fiscal
conservatives.
From starry skies and moonlit nights.
I am a child of God and a lover of life.
From another Galaxy, beyond the black holes,
trying to find home,
I am chicken and biscuits, pork and kraut.
I am delighted to be on planet Earth, but know
there's more.
I am searching and will find my place —- in time.

205

Pear Blossom Alley

Early spring   driving north on Santa Barbara
Street
     pass the Historical Museum
Over on the right
     glorious flowering pear trees
Ballet dancers en pointe
     frozen in fifth position
     limbs reach skyward
          dotted with lacy tulle petals
     hold aloft a crown of pure white petals
     legs, long, lithe
          twist together trunk-like
               Nature's symmetry
Santa Ana winds...
dainty blossoms swirl ... twirl ....whirl
                    white snow flurries
                    Nature's kaleidoscope

Beth Thompson

San Jose Del Cabo or "No hablo, Espanol"
by Margaret Roff

August, 1986. After completing my Executor duties after the death of my parents, I decide I need to get away to a quiet place to rest.

I find a travel agent and tell him, "I would like to go to a place that has sea and mountains, but not Hawaii as I lived there for six months."

He replies without hesitation, "You should go to Baja. I know a reasonably priced motel located on the beach." He makes reservations for the airplane and lodging.

I buy a copy of *God and Mr. Gomez*, by Jack Smith and a Berlitz Spanish book. The Berlitz book has phrases in Spanish organized by activity, i.e., dining, shopping. My sister comments, "The clerks won't want to wait while you look up each word in Spanish." In fact, she is wrong, the clerks seem not to care that I do this.

I pack lightly with only one change of clothing. I can easily pick up shirts and slacks in Baja. I approve of the motel that the travel agent selected with a swimming pool in the middle of the complex. I can hear the waves coming in when I lie down to sleep.

Each morning I take the cab into town. I say to the taxicab driver, "El banco, por favor." The bank is in the center town. There is a long line but no one seems impatient. I exchange my cash each day for pesos.

After exploring San Jose del Cabo and Los Cabos, I decide to drive to La Paz for a day trip. I take the cab to the airport six miles from San Jose del Cabo and rent a car from Hertz. I drive back to town, look at the gas gauge which is on empty.

I pull into the gas station and the attendant says, "I don't have any gas. The truck doesn't arrive until this afternoon sometime. The only other gas station in town does not have any gas either."

There are children playing outside the gas station. One of the older children helps me with placing a call to Hertz. The Hertz agent instructs me to return to the airport where he will help me.

I have no idea if the car can make it six miles on an empty tank, but I do not seem to have any options. It does make it.

At the airport, I explain to the agent that there is no gas in the tank. He assures me that the car will be ready. Behind me is a well-dressed business man from Guadalajara. I explain my predicament to him. He is kind enough to translate for me; they are getting another car for me and that the agent did not comprehend what I had said. He talks to the Agent and the car is soon ready.

The road to La Paz is a two lane road with little traffic. It is a beautiful drive with the mountains in the distance. I stop to buy a cold soda at the only store that I pass and I only see a small section of La Paz. On the return route, there are views of the ocean.

The plane going home was filled with tourists loaded down with packages. The Berlitz Spanish book and *God and Mr. Gomez,* turned out to be the right choice, as was Baja.

Dwell and Reflect

by Barry Shulman

Dwell upon your proudest deeds
Reflect upon your inner self
Pierce the vanity it breeds
And find the essence of all wealth

Look upon your finest side
Meditate on mirrored walls
Starve this thing that Man calls pride
Then drink the peace that soon befalls

Think how rich you deem your soul
Then bring to mind your self-deceit
A polished stone's a feeble goal
To love oneself equates retreat

I speak these words of humble thought
As if it's what I've always known
Yet praise the words this pen has brought
I've yet to harvest what I've sown.

Spring

by Gerson Kumin

Spring has come, or has it? According to the calendar it has, but not according to the weather. California tradition is that it rains in the winter and is hot in the summer. I ask, why in the season in between, are we getting winter weather?

A number of my friends who are allergic to pollen have assured me that Spring is here.

Perhaps they are right.

Then why is it raining?

I think that I shall rejoice in the rain. It will help to keep the pollen down. It also will help those of us who are concerned about drought.

Since "April Showers bring May Flowers", I guess we are halfway there since the flowers are already here. Even if they are March flowers. With their being here, I might as well accept that Spring has sprung.

Coupon

by Frank Warren

The word is old French meaning cut off a piece of paper which, I would say, makes the word a verb that, like Viking, became a noun. Coupons can be part of investment plans; you cut one off and trade it for money.

An old jingle goes something like this: "When you hear the radio announcing that you've got your wings of tin you can bet the Junior Birdmen have sent their coupons in."Or, if you prefer, "box tops."

I would love to carry on but I've got to send some coupons in for some swell prizes!

He Brought Me Red Roses

by Joyce Metz

My husband, Bill, brought me three red roses every Saturday. He was a traveling salesman who would be away from home two or three days — almost every week.

Bill would arrive home Fridays in time for dinner, but early Saturday mornings he selected new fabrics for the upholstered furniture at the factory where it was manufactured. On his way home for lunch Bill would stop at the florist's. He brought me three red roses every Saturday for thirty-five years.

Another sweet thing about Bill was when he left for a road trip he would write a short note and tuck it under my pillow. At bedtime, without fail, I'd find the little love note. Only once, as a joke, I stuck a note in his luggage.

Did I tell you he brought me red roses?

Bill never left the dinner table without telling me how good the meal was. Heck, it could have been leftovers or some new recipe I tried out. Didn't bother him. I always got a compliment.

Did I tell you he brought me red roses?

When Bill was home he was great with our two kids. He'd take them for haircuts, coach Billy's Little League team, buy them ice cream cones and teach Holly's Sunday School class. A good poppa.

Did I tell you I prefer yellow roses?

Summertime

by Suzanne Yoast - Perko

Lucky dogs! All those people who had summer homes at Yost Lake, a few miles from town. It was 1952 and I was 13 years old. We'd been living in Stillwater Oklahoma for several years. After moving a jillion times, finally we'd settled down for good. Anyway, as I was saying, Yost Lake was a special place. Mostly doctors, lawyers and bankers bought summer homes there, not exactly cabins for roughing it, but beautiful places with all the amenities.

The really great thing about Yost Lake was the entertainment area just across the lake. There were rowboats to use anytime you felt like it. There was a large wooden dance pavilion built out over the water with a multi-colored glass jukebox. It lit up and played all our favorite '50s music.......when you put a coin in it, of course. The sides of the pavilion were built so they could be propped open on a hot summer day to let the breeze in and the music out. You could hear it as it drifted across the water.

There was a very high metal slide on the water's edge. You picked up speed as you zoomed down it, wild, but fun. Further out in the lake was a large green wooden raft. My girlfriends and I loved to swim out there and work on our tans, relaxing and discussing our latest crushes. In junior high they changed often.

One day when we were hanging out on the raft, the other girls got bored and swam back to shore, but I stayed, soaking up the sun. Finally, I realized I was getting fried. I got up, tucked my hair into my swim cap, and went to dive off the raft and head back......Lo and behold! My eyes almost bugged out of my head! "Snake! Snake!" My friends were screaming! There it was, black and slimy, slithering through the water, close to the raft.

I was terrified! I'd never seen one out there before. My whole body was covered with goosebumps and the hair on my head felt like it was standing on end. I had a horrifying thought! Did Oklahoma have water moccasins?! How on earth was I going to get back to shore without being bitten or having the snake wrap around my leg?! I was practically hypnotized by it. I'd seen too many scary movies about people in swamps getting bitten by water moccasins!

I watched the snake glide through the water between me and the shore. Thank goodness he wasn't headed for the raft! He was headed for the pilings under the pavilion. After the snake was far enough away, I dove in and dog paddled as fast as I could to shore. Needless to say, my girlfriends and I weren't anxious to swim in Yost Lake for quite some time.

The View from Here

Squabble

by Marge Sweet Livingstone

You can't do that! You already counted the premium word squares in your previous turn.

I put an "s" on the end of poke making it a new word, so I can too count the premium squares again.

No you can't. Look it up.

OK, you're right.

Quirt is not a word!

Are you challenging me?

Yes I am.

Look it up.

Okay so it *is* a word.

It means 'to strike with a riding whip,' and you lose a turn.

You're putting an "s" on quirt? Well so am I, using my blank tile as an "s." Squirts.

You can't use a blank as an "s".

Are you challenging me again?

Yes.

Look it up.

Okay. I lose another turn.

Furthermore, 'squirts' uses seven tiles giving me a 50 point bonus.

No it doesn't. You must play all seven at once. Look it up.

Okay, you're right.

Honestly, don't you think this game should be called, 'Squabble?'

Squabble! Is that a word?

Look it up.

Uncle Bu

by Raven Wolfe

Some people are marked. No one knows why, it is simply a fact. In a family of five children, although they are each touched with something that makes them unique, there can be one, perhaps the second oldest, that is blighted in some manner; destined to stand out in a way that never allows him to fit snugly into the fabric of the familial brood. That is what happened to my uncle.

I don't know which of my memories are pure and which are tainted by the stories that float around my family, like mosquitoes softly buzzing in my ears. Stories of my Uncle Bu abound, like the legends of the old west or the ancient myths of Greece. I know (because I have heard, or overheard, this particular account a million and one times) that they realized something was seriously wrong with Uncle Bu on Christmas morning in 1975. This is not only a family legend, but a neighborhood legend.

Apparently, Uncle Bu woke up early that morning, took off all his clothes and went outside to walk up the street with his arms open as if embracing the rising sun. My grandfather, supposedly, ran after him, carrying a gray woolen blanket to cover Bu's nakedness. This occurred before I was born, but I have heard the story so many times it is as if I was there watching it all unfold. My grandmother, in her green bathrobe and bare feet, legend has it, stood on the front lawn wringing her hands, her hair dripping pink curlers onto the grass. Everyone says that at that very moment she changed from a young middle aged woman into a haggard old lady. Uncle Bu was 23, just home from Vietnam.

This is how my father describes the incident. "That stupid somabitch just marched up the goddamned street butt ass neked like he was Jesus H. Christ himself. All the neighbors was hangin' out their windows and laughin' their asses off. I had such a hangover from partying the night before that I could hardly see straight, but I did see his skinny ass prancing.....″ According to all accounts this occurred around 6 a.m., so the part about all the neighbors hanging out their windows is suspect.

My father is the second youngest, the last son. At the time of the Christmas morning event he was 16. He claims that Uncle Bu's naked display fucked up the remainder of his stint in high school. Strange events become the juiciest bit of gossip in a small town and everyone referred to him as Flasher's Brother. Any problem my father suffers gets blamed on his crazy brother – his lack of success with women, his financial and work difficulties, his chronic sinus condition, his alcoholism…

I have a picture of Uncle Bu holding me right after I was born. My grandmother is hovering over him, her arms out to catch me just in case Uncle Bu takes it into his head to drop me or throw me or something. Uncle Bu's face looks surprised and his blue eyes are focused on me, his lips pursed. He is saying booo at me. No one wanted him to hold me but my mom insisted. She said she always felt sorry for Uncle Bu and she knew he would never hurt anything or anyone.

Schizophrenia has robbed my uncle of his grasp on reality and it has robbed his body of grace. Now, in his late forties, my uncle walks with a forward lumber, his head and neck stiff, his arms unbending, his foot flexed upward. He lives in a group home in town, but when he is feeling well he stays with my grandparents out in the suburbs. They let him stay for a week or two or three and we get to watch him slowly deteriorate, silently measuring the darkness overtake him in tiny increments until he, is again, a familiar stranger who acts like he doesn't know us anymore. He sits on the brick wall in front of the house, hunched over and chain smoking as he talks to perhaps the sidewalk, the ants, his shoes. No one knows.

I know a lot about my uncle because when I was ten years old, my parents split up. They decided that my sister should live with my mother and since I am a boy, I should live with my father. My mom and my older sister got an apartment and my dad and I moved in with my grandparents and the occasional Uncle Bu. They keep his room for him and during his visits home, we gauge his deterioration by the smell that creeps under the door to his room. As his grasp on reality slips, so does his personal hygiene. At night, I hear my grandmother listing the signs of deterioration in a whining voice – the talking to himself, answering questions no one has asked, swatting at something unseen in the air around him, twitching, and the garbled speech that goes on and on, as if he is having a conversation with an invisible person.

Each time Uncle Bu comes home, he seems happy and strong and he talks a mile a minute about all kinds of things. My uncle is very intelligent and reads about five books a week. He knows everything about everything that happened in World War ll – the details of every battle, every German plane, every American General, every treaty signed, every speech made by Winston Churchill, each turn of events from the beginning to the end. He has shelves and shelves filled with war books and stacks of photos of bombed-out cities. Berlin, London, Amsterdam, Paris. He almost seems like a normal uncle, asking me about school, wanting to see my textbooks, talking about the videos he's rented. He walks with me up to the end of the street to watch me and my friends shoot baskets. The only thing giving away his hidden secret of insanity is his stiff lumbering walk. My grandfather says it's from all the meds he has to take.

My grandfather, always happy to see Uncle Bu, smiles a lot and asks him a lot of questions, as if he can pull him out of the web of his disease. My grandmother, who has never smiled in my presence as long as I can remember, ignores my uncle. Her pursed lips speak to everyone but Bu, as if his damage might be contagious simply by acknowledging his presence. Uncle Bu ignores her as well. He calls her Ma behind her back, but never addresses her directly.

Unfortunately, the deterioration creeps into him, like a shadow crossing the sun. His clear pale eyes turn darker each day; he smokes more and more cigarettes and paces back and forth in front of the house. His smoker's cough deepens and he mumbles to himself. Eventually he turns ugly and stiff and almost spastic in his movements. It's usually my grandmother that says the words.

"It's time for him to leave, Frank. Time for him to go back to that place." She says this to my grandfather, whose job it is to gently tell my uncle he has to return to his residential treatment center. During the last few days of each visit my grandmother spends a lot of time in her bedroom rearranging the bottles on her dresser, the shoes in her closet, the tiny shell shaped soaps in a dish in her bathroom. She allows Uncle Bu to visit for my grandfather's sake. If it were her choice, her son would never be welcome in her home.

My grandfather is a saint. He puts up with my grandmother's silences and mood swings. The only thing he insists on is that Uncle Bu is always welcome to come home when he is in a good period. That is all he seems to desire anymore. He and my grandmother act like strangers. They sleep in separate beds and I never see them touch. When Uncle Bu is home my grandfather, who keeps himself busy with projects that usually involve one of his cars or his boat, makes feeble attempts to get my uncle interested in what he is doing.

Each time he has to take my uncle back to town to his group home, my grandfather's long narrow face becomes deeply lined and his eyes have a look of despair. He opens the door of his van and puts his hand on Bu's back, as if he is helping Bu lift himself into the high seat. Bu seems fragile next to my grandfather. His eyes are hooded in suspicion and his long hands tremble. He sits, bent and resigned, staring into space, not looking at anything. Sometimes he mumbles repetitive phrases over and over. "Lucy in the sky with diamonds Lucy in the sky with diamonds Lucy in the sky with diamonds." Sometimes he hums notes in no particular order, forming no particular tune. Anything to quiet the voices in his head.

All his nieces and nephews call him Bu, although his given name is Ron. My older cousins started it long before I was born. Apparently, when we were little he would address us each as Boo, perhaps because he couldn't remember our names or perhaps it's a symptom of his illness. When I was in first grade I drew a picture of my family. There are five of us – my dad with sticky hair pointing out of the top of his head, my mom with huge circular shoes, my sister Jaralyn, with green hands that look like mittens, me half as large as everyone else and way off to the side of the paper, Uncle Bu holding a triangle with the word "bu" written in faint pencil. My mom bought a cheap frame and stuck the picture in it and hung it in the kitchen. When the family broke up she wanted to keep it, but I insisted that it was mine and she let me have it.

My sister comes to visit us on Sundays and my mom picks me up every Wednesday night for dinner. My sister's in city college now and I'm starting classes there next year after I graduate. Jaralyn reminds me of my grandmother; her mouth a straight solemn line and her arms always folded over her chest. We rarely talk to each other and when she visits on Sundays she brings a backpack full of books, which means she's always occupied with something.

Sunday is the day the aunts and uncles and cousins descend on my grandparents. They swarm in, eat everything they can, sneak a few beers, which they have to bring since my grandparents don't allow alcohol in their home and then leave all at once, like a cloud of locusts. Most of the cousins are much older than I am, some of them have little kids. The house is full of noise, the back yard filled with small children running around eating popsicles. My cousin Roy and I usually go up the street to shoot baskets and his kids come with us to chase the ball for Roy because he's really fat and doesn't like to move too much. Sometimes we walk up to the creek and smoke a joint. I don't think he's ever said more to me than "So, how ya doin?" No matter what I respond, he says the same thing. "Oh. Cool, man. That's cool." I could tell him my penis had just turned green. "Oh. Cool, man. That's cool." I could tell him I just won the Nobel Prize for astrophysics. "Oh. Cool, man. That's cool." I don't ask him how he's doing. I'm afraid it would tax his brain.

During these Sunday visits my grandmother becomes a frantic mess, wringing her hands, shooing kids out of her flower beds, fussing over handprints on the doors and table tops. She is a warden, stalking the property, suspiciously seeking out unpermitted sitting on certain chairs or touching items that are deemed "off limits."

"Christie, get your hands off grandma's vase," I will hear one of my aunts yell. "Hey, Buck, you can't sit on the white couch. Remember what Grandma said?" In the midst of all the commotion, my grandfather beams silently and watches the grandchildren take over the house and the garden. He doesn't talk much but his eyes always let you know what he's feeling. On Sundays he is simply happy. The rest of the week, he spends most of his time doing some project in the garage, under the hood of a car, reorganizing the piles of magazines, restacking cans of old paint, inspecting endless hammers and vice grips and pliers. His latest thing is pulling clover in the middle of the night. He wears a miner's light on his head and crawls around the front yard on his hands and knees with a digging implement and a plastic bag. Maybe it's no wonder my Uncle Bu is crazy.

If Uncle Bu happens to be home on Sunday he avoids the tumult. He usually sits in his favorite spot – the brick wall out front. He smokes incessantly, staring into space, watching the kids run back and forth, nodding and smiling, calling the little ones Boo. Most of his nieces and nephews are afraid of him and rumors abound. They claim he eats small animals, that he is a devil worshipper, that if he catches you alone he will put a spell on you. My sister Jaralyn is the only one who acknowledges him. At some point she will sidle up to him and kiss him on the cheek and whisper "Boo" in his ear. My uncle likes when she does this and chuckles. When we were little she liked to sit in his lap and let him stroke her long blond hair. My mother always reminded us to be nice to Uncle Bu. She was the only one in the family not afraid of him, the only one able to see his essence behind all the strange mannerisms.

By the time the Sunday onslaught is over (no one stays longer than two hours), my grandmother is a trembling mess with a headache, shrieking at my grandfather about the disorder in the house. My dad avoids the whole family scene. He is usually gone on a long errand, on a supposed date with a woman none of us has ever met, or perhaps visiting friends that we all doubt exist. I think that being in his 40's and living with his parents is starting to affect him.

My relationship with Bu is difficult to define. We rarely acknowledge each other. As a young child I believed all the crazy stories my cousins told me about him. When I got older, my mom talked to me about him. "Your Uncle isn't as crazy as he makes out to be. He's just too sensitive for this family. Don't be afraid of him. He wouldn't hurt a flea. No one understands him. They all think he's stupid or something. Honey, your uncle is one of the smartest people I know. Someone had to turn out crazy in that family. It just happened to be him, although, I hate to say it, your father's probably number two on the list of crazies."

I saw how she was with him, how she would sit on the brick wall next to him and talk to him for long periods of time. Sometimes they exchanged books and sometimes she would bring him brownies she had baked especially for him.

When she and my dad decided to split up I saw her sitting with Bu blowing her nose, his hand stiffly patting her on the back. I think the whole family's a total loss in the mental health department.

One day I was in town with some guys, driving up and down looking for some kind of action. We must have driven by the group home where Uncle Bu lives because I saw him sitting on the front steps of a big old house that looks just like I imagined a group home would look – old, dilapidated, scraped paint chips on the stucco. He sat hunched over, smoking frantically and rocking back and forth. "Hey" one of my friends said. "Isn't that your uncle?" I pretended I hadn't seen him. I was ashamed. He looked wildly crazy – crazier than he ever looks when he comes for visits. Having a mildly crazy uncle is OK, it's something that makes me unique to my friends. But this uncle, the rocking, gesticulating, stick figure man surrounded by billows of smoke and stamping his feet – I simply couldn't claim him as a family member.

"Who? That guy? That guy right there? Hell, no. He's not my uncle. No, it may look like him but it's not him. Bu's not that crazy." I haven't seen him since. He hasn't been home in several months and we expect him to call any day now to tell us that he's feeling better and would like to come home. I know my grandfather will beam at the news, that my grandmother will wring her chapped hands and shake her head from side to side, that my father will sigh deeply and mutter something insulting under his breath. As for me, I have come to accept Bu's occasional presence. Maybe someday I'll be like Jaralyn and be able to sit and talk to him. Maybe someday when I drive by his group home and see him sitting on the steps rocking back and forth and spewing to the air around him, I will be able to wave at him or even stop and go give him a high five. Maybe I won't be ashamed of him and if not that, I may be able to forgive myself for being ashamed of him.

Last Year I
by Mary Frink

Last year I

wrote a report

edited a book

grieved a loss

comforted a friend

inhaled art

feared for our country

loved unconditionally

Life after World War II - London
by Rosita Arbagey

There'll always be an England,
And England shall be free
If England means as much to you
As England means to me.

LONDON: World War ll ended in Europe May 8, 1945. I was 13 years old at the time, passing through Trafalgar Square in London with my mother. There were a few people loitering around the square. Some were sitting on the fountain, and others were feeding the pigeons. Suddenly there were loud yells of "The War is Over!" Big Ben, the big clock in the tower that sits above the Palace of Westminster where the British Parliament meets, began booming. Mother started crying as did other people who hugged and kissed each other. This was totally out of character for the British, but soon there was a great surge of people coming out of offices, the tube stations, and buses, including the drivers and the conductors who left the public transportation at a standstill.

American and British soldiers and civilians were jumping into the fountains, and pretty soon, you could not move as there were so many bodies swirling around. We arrived home very late and very tired, having had to walk most of the way, pushing our way through throngs of people who were celebrating. When we arrived home, we were greeted by neighbors and strangers who sang and danced in the street.

"Knees Up Mother Brown,
When the Lights come on again,
Daisy, Daisy, Give me your answer do,
Red, White and Blue,
Land of Hope and Glory,
Bumpsy Daisy,

The View from Here

Oh! What a lovely bunch of coconuts,
and
The Lambeth Walk "

People were getting drunk, either with spirits or elation, until the wee hours of the morning. The following weekend, people organized victory parties in the streets. Neighbors who never thought of speaking to one another during a normal day dragged out chairs and tables, and covered them with the British flag. The weather favored us; it turned out to be a warm spring day. People made costumes out of the Union Jack, and prizes were given for the best outfit. Everywhere you saw red, white and blue, the colors of the flag. Whatever food they had to spare, they shared with everyone. We did not know that rationing would continue for some time. We tasted marvelous dishes made of spam (a war time processed meat sent from America), and pastries made from mineral oil and whatever other food stuffs people had hoarded in case of desperate times.

Father served in the 8th Army under General Montgomery. After the invasion of Italy, he was assigned to an Internment Camp at Terni, Italy where quite a few prominent political Italians were interned, including Mussolini's wife and two of her children. Father told Mother he wanted her to take me out of school as soon as I became of age, which was 14 at that time, rather than waiting for me to matriculate. He wanted us to join him in Italy because we had been separated for so many years that we were more like strangers than family. In addition, I would get a once-in-a-lifetime education of past and present history, geography, and different cultures. Mother was delighted that she would soon be in her element as an Army wife. This meant I had to finish one more miserable year at the Carlisle School for Girls. The only time I felt I belonged there, was when I smuggled in a book I found under Mother's bed. It was the first so-called erotic book of that era called *Forever Amber*. Mother did not read during the day, only at night. To her, to read during the day was a sign of laziness. I knew if I was caught bringing the book to school, I would be expelled. I sneaked it out at break time, and covered it with the jacket of one of our school books. I became part of the popular girls' group as they sat around me on the lawn and listened as I read each chapter. In retrospect I felt like Scheherazade. When I reached home, I would quickly replace it under my mother's bed, of which I was glad she never found out. The year passed slowly but finally it came to an end. I was happy to say Goodbye to Miss Finney and the school for good.

The Airport
by Brian Silsbury

It was one of those glorious Indian summer mornings that you long for but rarely experience. Chichi, a good sailing friend and I were lazing in the quaint old Santa Barbara Airport gardens. We had checked in early for the San Francisco flight and were waiting for our boarding announcement. Small aircraft buzzed around the airfield like worker bees foraging for nectar. I was content and relaxed.

Our flight plan was to visit Peter, an old friend who had recently moved his goods and chattels to Victoria, British Colombia. I started to fidget.

"We ought to go through to the departure lounge," I suggested.

"No, let's wait until they call the flight."

Almost on cue, the loud speaker crackled into life. "This is the final call for UA4234 United flight

251

to San Francisco. All passengers must proceed to the departure lounge, Gate 8 immediately."

"Final call, there must be some mistake. This is the first announcement I've heard from United," I said anxiously, my tranquility shattered. We gathered up our hand luggage and rushed to the departure gate. To my dismay, there were six people already waiting for security clearance. As we joined the line, the female security official smiled and greeted the next man as she took his passport and boarding pass. Feeling anxious I tried to butt in, "Ah, excuse me, United has just made the final boarding call for the San Francisco flight, can we move to the front of the line please?"

The woman's head swiveled from the man to me, winning smile—off. Her steely eyes bore into me. "No. You will wait in line."

"But they've called our flight," I pleaded.

She was unmoved. "I don't care, stand in line." She turned back to the man, winning smile—on. "Everything is in order sir, move in front of him," and indicated that he should move ahead of me. This time they called us by name. "Will Mr. Silsbury and Mrs. Stanford board the aircraft immediately?" There's that action word *'immediately'* again, I squirmed. Chichi was beginning to get anxious too and interceded, but only managed to make the security woman even angrier.

By now I was really hot under the collar. I'd been spaced out in the airport gardens for nearly two hours and was about to miss my flight because the miserable speaker system had chosen not to work.

The security woman took my travel documents.

"Your earlier announcements didn't come through in the gardens. Are you sure you made them?" I asked timidly.

"I've made the announcements for all the flights. They *are* broadcast throughout this terminal. In any case, you are required to be in the departure lounge at least thirty minutes before the scheduled take off." She growled, as if by rote.

Moving closer to the X-ray machine and metal detector, an uncharitable thought about the gargoyle like security woman came unbidden into my mind; I wouldn't want her jackboots under my bed!

As I tried to wait patiently, I noted that none of the other travelers had the compassion to let us move to the front. The dreadful security woman had scared them all.

"Take off your shoes and coat, put them in a tray. Any metal in your pockets, keys, mobile phones? Put them in the tray," barked the security man.

I threw my passport and boarding pass into the tray along with my bits of metal. The detector awoke as I walked through. "Buzz" went its alarm like an angry hornet about to stick its long barbed sting into my neck.

"Take off your belt and wrist watch."

I took off the watch and left my belt on. I'd

never had a problem with the belt before. It was to be my second mistake of the afternoon. "Buzz" went the detector again.

"I told you to take off your belt, now stand over there," said the security man.

No wonder my blood pressure gets high. I'm on the final boarding call and now I've earned a full body scan. Where the hell is the scan man with his magic wand? I spot him inspecting an aluminum walking frame. I assumed it belonged to a little old lady, bent over with arthritis, hovering nearby. She struggled to keep her balance by holding the back of a chair. I swear she must be in her nineties. The scan man obviously thinks she is a big security risk! I watch, fascinated as he removed the rubber feet from the bottom of the walker and peered into its tubular frame.

The speaker blares out our names again: "Silsbury and Sanford, go to the aircraft *now*!" Clearly, they had given up on the word **immediately** as a motivational adverb. Chichi was through security and waiting for me. Nodding, I suggested she go on but she declined.

The little old lady was finally cleared and moved out of the way. Now it was my turn.

Again, I got the "buzz" from the scan man's metal detector.

"Take off your belt sir," he demanded. I yanked the belt from around my waist and he tried again; this time, all was quiet. Chichi moved off to the aircraft as the dreaded speaker sputtered into life again. "Silsbury to rebook on a later flight, luggage will be taken off the aircraft." My heart would have sunk into my shoes had I been wearing them.

I fastened my belt and laced up my shoes. Then a wave of panic! There was no sign of my passport or boarding pass in the tray! Chichi must have picked them up I hoped desperately. She was now on her way to a long-suffering, and trifle hoarse, flight attendant. I rushed to the gate where two members of the ground staff chatted amiably. I could see Chichi had almost reached the aircraft. I shouted from the door but she didn't hear me; she marched on, oblivious to my plight. For once, the staff was lenient, and let me through without a boarding pass. Running to the aircraft, I just got to the steps as Chichi was about to board.

"I hope you've got my travel documents," I gasped.

"Yes, they're here. Wait a minute, I mistakenly gave them your boarding pass instead of mine and they accepted it," she grinned. So much for tight security, I thought, as I entered the cabin, garnering glares from my fellow passengers.

I flopped into the seat next to Chichi, closed my eyes and finally relaxed. Almost immediately the reassuring 'thud and clunk' filtered into my semi-somnolent state as the cabin door was shut and locked by the flight attendant. I could hear the starboard engine cough a couple of times, then burst into life. Its portside twin protested, then came alive shortly after.

"Good morning folks, this is Captain

257

Culpepper from the flight deck." The overhead speakers went quiet for a couple of minutes then crackled back to life. "Bad news I am afraid. San Francisco Air Traffic Control has just informed me that fog has enveloped the airport. We are instructed to remain here until further notice."

The Ice Truck

by Suzanne Yoast-Perko

When I was seven, my family moved to Henderson, Kentucky into a furnished upstairs apartment. Mother was very unhappy to find there was an antiquated icebox, not the usual modern refrigerator. But my older brother and I were delighted! Mother would put a small cardboard sign in the living room window indicating the amount of ice we needed: 25, 50, or 70 pounds.

The iceman came by several times a week. On Saturday afternoon the neighborhood kids were excited to see the truck headed our way. His truck had an open wooden bed filled with lots of huge rectangular shaped blocks of ice, covered with a giant tarp to help keep them frozen. When he uncovered the ice, we were standing close by watching the process as he used his icepick to chip off just the right sized block to fit into the upper section of our icebox. He used huge metal tongs with a large hook on each end to clamp onto the big square chunk of ice.

When he headed up the stairs to our apartment, the kids would lean over the end of the truck bed on their tiptoes and gather up the ice chips, large and small. They were especially enjoyable on a hot summer day! If it was really roasting out, we'd follow the truck around on his route for a few blocks and continue to help ourselves to the leftover ice chunks.

Thank goodness the delivery man was a good hearted soul. He got a kick out of us eating the chips of ice and following the truck around the neighborhood. He probably remembered doing the same thing when he was a little kid.

Ah, the simple joys of summer in the "good old days"......

Fame

by Douglas Huston

Neil was famous for traveling a

long way - getting out of his vehicle

walking around a little

and going home.

Muhammed was famous for floating like a

butterfly and stinging like a bee.

Jesse was famous for running in

circles quickly

Diana was famous for swimming in the Atlantic

and swimming and swimming

Orville and Wilbur were famous

for flying just that

Fred was famous for being light on

his feet

Ginger was famous for doing it all in reverse

Johnny was famous for making us laugh late at

night

Seychelle, my very young friend

is famous for melting hearts

with her smile

I Remember When......
by Barbara Godley

Campbell tomato soup was 10 cents a can
a movie ticket was 25 cents, popcorn 10

Hiking in the hills with my sister, friends and
dog,

swimming in lakes and rivers on family
vacations,

dancing in our nightgowns on warm windy
evenings in the front yard.

All good memories
I collect more and more memories as life goes on,

but my childhood memories stay with me and
and I go back and refer to them when times are
difficult,

I'll leave the difficult times and keep the fun times
going.

Where do They Come From?
by Douglas Huston

The last one clung to the outside of my spaceship
for a free ride to earth

The crowd outside the gate was created when a
virus went bad

One was sewn together from spare parts and
infused with lightning

Still more appear from strange plants that grow
too quickly from the ground

Another appears only when the full moon is
showing bright

And some go around biting others in the dark of
night

Some are too coincidentally discovered in the
frozen ice and defrosted

Another waits in a lake for unsuspecting tourists
with bad cameras

And one or two angry ones live only in Japan

Now they hide in the shadows and wait

Or live in the closet

Or under my bed!

An Intrusion

by Joan E. Jacobs

"BOO!"

"You don't scare me anymore, you disgusting arachnid. Go back up to your filthy nest and leave me alone."

"My, my aren't we testy?"

"You're invading my space."

"So? It isn't the first time and it probably won't be the last."

"If you're not careful, it could be your last. Now, as I've said before, leave me alone. I've got a lot of thinking to do."

"That's a first – you thinking. What are you thinking about?"

"If you must know, my love life has been on the decline."

"No wonder! Have you looked at yourself lately in the mirror? All the curds and whey you have been eating certainly hasn't done anything to your tuffet."

"I heard Georgie Porgie like's girls with a little meat on them."

"Georgie Porgie – that lowlife? He kisses the girls and then leaves them. What kind of guy is that? Now I heard Wee Willie Winkie isn't a bad guy."

"Are you kidding? I don't want to wait all night for a guy while he makes sure all those little monsters are in bed. Peter, Peter Pumpkin Eater is single again, I heard."

"Do you know why his wife left him? Do you? He made her live in a pumpkin. What kind of life is that?"

"Who is there then? Little Boy Blue wouldn't be much fun. He does nothing all day but sleep. I certainly wouldn't want to date Jack Horner. He's always sitting in a corner. Jack be Nimble might be fun if he wasn't always jumping over things. It's so darn frustrating."

"I like girls that are a little on the plump side. How about me?"

"Are you out of your mind? I wouldn't be seen dead with a varmint like you! Ugh!"

"Kiss me. You might be surprised. I'm really not what I seem."

"I'm not sure I'm that desperate."

"What do you have to lose?"

"Yuck! Phooey! You're nothing but a dirty old spider. I'm going to sue you for harassment."

"What did you expect, a prince? Only frogs turn into princes after they're kissed. I heard there's a good-looking one down at the pond. You better hurry though. I heard Little Bo Peep is eyeing him. From all reports, she's darn tired looking after all those damn sheep."

Spring Cleaning

by Douglas Huston

I had a thought. It was more of an idea. A good one, I'm sure. But now I can't find it. It was right here next to the grocery list and that quote I was keeping in my head to tell a friend later. Maybe if I backtrack through my thought process I can find it. Let's see, a moment ago I was standing by the window looking out at the trees and…and what? Thinking about that time on the lake, or was I planning a trip to the lake?

There's an awful lot going on in here. Maybe if I did some organizing and let a few things go I could find the stuff I do need. I could organize all the memories of all the dogs I've had in my life, keep them in one file. Forget all the bad things they did (like chewing up those nice shoes from

Italy and chasing a porcupine) and keep all the good memories of hikes and joyfully chasing everything on the beach.

I remember now. I was thinking about how I used to climb trees a lot as a kid. I was good at it and could size up a tree in a moment. I was trying to remember when that stopped and why. That tree I was looking at is a good climbing tree. I could test it out. Or maybe not.

Back to cleaning. Over here in the corner is a pile of memories about high school so could probably let those go. Near that is a partial memory of my sister and her creepy boyfriend back then. I wonder what happened to the rest of it. Maybe mixed in with all that weird family stuff that I really don't want to try and sort out just now. Some other time.

In the back is a partial picture of the girl I fell in love with in the first grade. I still remember her name. Why am I hanging on to that? It sits all by itself, not crowded with a lot of other junk. Not like that messy pile over there of all the

272

relationships from my teens and beyond. And the exes, hmmm, maybe I'll put those over with the family stuff for another time.

The birds outside the window certainly are going on, trying to tell me something, but what? I remember the parakeet we had when I was a kid. Blue, or yellow. Maybe we had more than one.

Look, here's a memory of where I left those tools I've been missing for a while. I wonder if that jacket I lost is in there? And my kayak! Wait, I still have my kayak. It sure is a nice day out. I could go kayaking.

I just remembered that I hate cleaning.

The View from Here

Christmas In Summerland

by Barbara Godley

When I was little, Christmas always meant a lot to me. When I was four my older cousin, Bill dressed up as Santa, rang bells at the back door, I believed. Years later another cousin put on the costume when my children were little and I couldn't believe that I actually thought it was Santa, Even my three year old wasn't fooled.

I may not believe in Santa anymore, but I believe in the spirit of Christmas and every year it brings joy into my life. In our family everyone brings something to the table. The host cooks the turkey and dressing, but the rest of the meal is brought by sisters, cousins, children, and grandchildren.

This year I enjoyed decorating the house, every room including the bathrooms had Christmas in them. I did little cooking as my older daughter came several days early. We had a day off on Friday and went to see art, a movie and out to dinner. The next day the cooking began. She makes the most wonderful desserts and she also brined the turkey. Later in the day my younger daughter arrived and started on the stuffing. Her

stuffing is a meal in itself as it contains nuts, sausage, fruit, homemade corn bread etc.

I don't have a big house and the living room on Christmas morning was filled with gifts. They covered the hearth, coffee table, couches, floor and were escaping into the hall. We had a great morning with a delicious breakfast and the turkey was in the oven by ten. However, we usually serve dinner by five, but it was a large turkey and would take longer, which made dinner an hour later than usual.

My granddaughter and kids arrived at 2:00 and more Christmas happened. We cleaned up all the paper, ribbon and boxes and the house looked normal for the four o'clock arrival of my sister, brother -in-law and niece and our cousin and two grown sons. More presents were opened, drinks and hors d' oeuvres served.

After dinner my cousin's son, John, played Christmas carols and my niece stood beside him and led us in song. It was a moving moment for me. Then came the reading of the "Night before Christmas", read by my great granddaughter, Reanen and the passing of the "50 centers." Every year we each bring an inexpensive gift for passing around. Some are store bought, some are white elephants and some are home made, and it is so much fun..

My four year old great grandson did not want to pass his gift on, but soon got into the game. Every time the word "the" is read the gift is passed and at the end you can exchange with someone else. And then the gifts are opened and what surprises are in store.

My daughters, granddaughter and great grandchildren stayed for several days and we had more Christmas Cheer and loving times.

Out My Back Door

by Douglas Huston

While I'm nestled in my old clamshell-backed metal rocker with the hand painted pastel green finish, sipping coffee, soaking up the sun and reading an engrossing book, something darts quickly past the edge of my vision. I look up to see a hummingbird inspecting the blooms that are everywhere on the succulents I grow in large pots. While I watch, another swoops down from nowhere to chase the first hummingbird. They are a mere four feet away, close enough to see the iridescent colors on their backs. Soon two more join in and then another two. It becomes a circus in the airspace just in front of me, swooping, diving, chasing straight up then back down as though I were not even there. One of the boldest zips over to me and briefly touches the book I'm holding with her beak. A greeting? I want to think so. A full ten minutes later they gradually slip away one by one. The show is over.

The chair sits just outside the back door of my little studio which itself sits among the oaks up in the foothills. One night I hear a rustling in the leaves and peek out to see a large skunk scavenging through the brush and though I turn the light on she is unperturbed. I watch for a while through the glass in my back door, my curiosity tempered by experience. A different morning reveals the rabbit that seems to live nearby and if I'm quiet and still he does his foraging uninterrupted. I know he knows that I am there.

Sometime last year I began hearing the strangest noises coming from just a short ways down, near the fallen oak. A sound that was something between a choking cat and an awkward growl. I go out with the flashlight and shine it down in the direction only to have the reflection of four or five pairs of eyes looking back at me. It takes a few nights to determine that it is a family of grey foxes. One particular night as I stand in the open doorway one of the adult foxes walks slowly out and across the edge of the tree line then straight up towards me stopping just a few feet away. For a full 30 seconds he stares at me and I stare back at him. Then he saunters back to his den and family.

I have often observed a fair-sized bobcat coming and going through the grounds, usually signaled by the cacophony of crows on the alert. The morning after the fox staring contest, the bobcat stood a few feet away and stared at me also, as though determining where I stood in the chain.

The crows, the resident owl, budgies, jays lizards and squirrels that race through the trees are all part of the backdrop to my wonderland, the Nature Channel that is out my back door.

The View from Here

St. Valentine's Ball

by Brian Silsbury

Shame on me, 21 and still a virgin!

Some say I am a good-looking guy; six feet, blond with blue eyes and an open face. I once overheard a couple of giggling girls whisper, "Look at his tight butt, hmm, not bad!"

My virginity is still there, but not for the want of trying, it's just that I am so damn shy. I even blush when a girl speaks to me. The word is out; I am painfully shy and inexperienced in the ways of dating.

Tonight I will be with my buddies at the Grand St. Valentine's Ball. I know what will happen; I ask a girl to rhumba, to quick step or foxtrot and she dances with me. When the music turns to a close and clingy waltz, she mumbles

283

under her breath and leaves me looking like a stranded whale, alone on the dance floor. I think girls are scared of being stuck with me and of missing opportunities with one of the sex-crazed Don Juans! My buddies make matters worse. They snuggle up with their latest conquest, laugh and share tales of my naivety, virginity and misfortune.

The St. Valentine's Ball changes everything. That is when Annemarie enters my life. She is more sultry and mature than the other girls and she intoxicates me with her dusky beauty and exotic perfume. I dance and nuzzle her long, curly, chestnut hair. When she speaks she has the unnerving habit of gazing directly into my eyes. I am out of control as she totally immerses me in her deep brown pools. Annemarie has a throaty chuckle which she uses to continually challenge me. She effectively puts me at ease so I am able to open my defenses and slowly overcome my shyness.

We dance well together and are possessive in

not allowing anyone else to cut in.

"Ladies and Gentlemen, please take your partner for the last waltz. We end the evening with that old Nat King Cole favorite – Unforgettable," announces the master of ceremonies signaling the end of the evening. We stand up as one and I reach for her hand. She smiles and smooths her rich, red dress grinning knowingly at her friends as we move to the dance floor.

I am in wonderland during the last waltz. We become so entwined we can hardly move and only shuffle thigh to thigh. I am very hot and very bothered which is a new and exciting experience for me. As we walk back to the table she whispers, "Would you like to come back to my home for a drink or coffee? My parents are visiting the family in Italy; they are away for a month."

I can hardly believe my ears. My mouth is dry and my guts are performing summersaults in anticipation. She says goodbye to her friends as we leave the dance hall holding hands. I smirk at my buddies as we pass their table and move out into the fresh air. At just five foot two, she comfortably slips under my arm as we head towards her home.

"Some of my girlfriends say you are very shy"

I blush as I think how right they are.

"I'm sure you will blossom in the right hands," she says with a wry smile.

Annemarie rummages in her purse for the front door day as we climb the stairs. Locking the door behind us, she guides me into the spacious living room. Pulling me in close, she gives me a deep and demanding kiss. I quickly respond, my hands running all the way down her back.

"My, oh my, your hands are lethal. It is years since I've felt like this."

Annemarie pulls herself away. "Why don't you take off your jacket and tie and kick off your shoes. Just make yourself comfortable on the sofa and yes, the bathroom is through that door." She nods in the direction of the hallway. "I'll go and

286

slip into something more casual." Grinning and still disbelieving my luck, her words and actions sound like an erotic movie script.

"Aaaaaggggaaa!" Annemarie's blood-curdling scream echoes from her bathroom and jerks me away from my fantasy. She dashes out, her normally dark complexion ghostly white. She has changed into an elegant pink, silk dressing gown which flies open from her headlong rush. I force myself to look into her eyes and not peep down. The gown is still open as I rush over and pull her trembling body close to mine.

"What is it? What is wrong?"

"There is a huge spider trapped in my bath! Get rid of it NOW! I hate all spiders especially ones with black hair." Still distressed, she is almost incoherent.

I push her backwards onto the sofa and run into her bathroom. Sure enough, the spider is big and desperate to escape up the smooth side of the bath. Although I'm not afraid of spiders, I would never, ever, touch this one. I pick up the wooden back-scrubber and am about to whack it into oblivion when I remember Buddha's compassionate saying. It flashes into my mind, probably after years of meditation.

"Do not kill any living thing. Let all beings be happy."

I grab Annemarie's hand towel and "fish" for the spider. The evil insect is a quick learner and soon climbs swiftly aboard the towel. To ensure it didn't continue its escape over my hand and up my arm, I give the towel a fast shake. The dislodged spider falls off and bolts under the bathroom cabinet.

A couple of minutes later I wander back into the living room and jauntily announce, "Okay, Annemarie, I've sorted it out."

She smiles, "Jamie, I am so sorry. That damn spider really frightened me and killed my passion."

"Bugger, what shitty luck; my night to remember has been ruined by a bloody great spider," I think bitterly!

I switch back to the room to hear Annemarie murmur, "Tomorrow is Sunday. Come here early evening. I'll fix a light supper and then we can really get to know each other."

The telephone shatters my deep and untroubled sleep. I reach over, turn on the light and check the time. Who the hell is calling me at 7 am on a Sunday? I grab the phone off the cradle.

"Jamie, you're a lying bastard! You said you'd killed the spider." Annemarie yells. She gasps for air and continues haranguing me.

"The spider is back in my bath. You didn't kill the bloody thing, you lily-livered wimp!"

"Is your invitation to a romantic supper still on tonight?" I ask meekly.

She slams the phone down.

"I guess not."

Mind Chatter

Coulda, woulda, shoulda
Mind chatter, empty words, failed
Intentions I could have done this.
I would have done
That. I should have…if only

If only…
Mind chatter, shaming and blaming
If only I had said, "I love you."
If only I had given you chances. But

But…
The ever present excuse word
But I didn't know
But I didn't mean to. I ought to have…

I ought to…
The doubtful dictum, oath to obligation.
You ought to toughen up.
You ought to grin and bear it.

Mind chatter. Mindless chatter.
Take those couldas, wouldas, shouldas
    together with onlys, buts, and ought-tos trash
    them, burn then.

Go ahead. First you cry
    Scream, rant and rave
Grieve,
      Then…
          Dream again.
             Hope again.
                Love yourself again.

Beth Thompson

Grand Central Market

by Douglas Huston

My job is to keep track of my little sister who is three. I am barely five and she's quick so it's a big job. We sit together on the hard wooden bench holding hands on what is one of the last of the Red Cars in Los Angeles. They are slowly being torn out, voiding LA of its connecting arteries, to be replaced with concrete. However, I don't know any of this, all I know is that the three of us are going on a big adventure. I look around at all the unusual faces riding with us, different than the faces I'm used to seeing in my small world in Altadena. I'm fascinated.

My mother is not tall, but walks fast and it is hard to keep up with her in the crowded streets. "Come on," I say to my little sister. Finally we get where we are going. Grand Central Market my mother tells us, and we enter the enormous, endless space that I later come to compare to Disneyland in all its wonder and excitement.

The first thing that hits me are the smells of people pushed close, the earthiness of fresh vegetables and butchered animals. They hang in sections on hooks and various parts are laid out in glass cases set down low at the perfect height for a five year old to observe up close. I forget my sister as I run from one to another, then back to grab her hand so I can share what I have just seen. I drag her over to see the pig's head staring up at us looking a little lost. We are too young to be scared or grossed out, we are happily at that wonderful stage of innocent awe. Next we go to the enormous cow's tongue, then on to plucked, headless chickens, someone's brain and other parts we know nothing about, but look a bit like things we have seen in old science fiction movies on television. We press up close to the glass and chatter back and forth about our discoveries.

Fish! All sizes and shapes of fish laying on their sides watching us with one large round eye. We giggle and rush to the next, odd things in shells. I see the small Chinese man behind one of the cases who notices us and smiles warmly. He must know that we are on a great adventure.

It suddenly occurs to me that I have lost my mother and I look up and around through the crowd. After a moment I spot her not far away calmly watching the two of us. She has a bag with a few items in it and leads us down to produce for more wonder and newness.

Our vocabulary is limited, my sister and I, but we make the most of it all the way home and that night our dreams are more colorful and vivid than ever before.

The Train Trip

by William Livingstone

In the winter of 1944-1945, during World War II, I was a POW at Stalag Luft IV POW camp near Stettin, Poland, located in a forested area near the Polish-German border, not far from the Baltic Sea. I was there for about two months when, in the last week of December, we heard artillery guns as the war between the Germans and the Russians moved closer to the German-Polish border.

On December 30th the word came down we would be evacuated from Stettin the following day, the destination to be another prison camp, Stalag XIII near Nuremberg, 300 miles to the southwest. Early the next morning our German guards issued each of us a Red Cross food parcel. With the crunch of crusty snow under our feet, we marched out of Stalag Luft IV to a nearby railroad siding where we climbed into rickety old boxcars.

A thin layer of straw lay on the rough wooden floor of our boxcar, but it did little to make us comfortable or warm. A five-gallon bucket provided our toilet. We were permitted to empty it only once a day. The Gerrys locked twenty-five of us in each car. Small by American standards, European boxcars measured only about 25 feet long, and about 7 feet wide. When we all sat down with our backs against the side walls and our legs extended, our feet would meet in the center -- sole to sole. For the most part, that's how we traveled, sitting on the floor side by side, occupying every bit of the floor space. To go to the bucket we had to step over and between a floor full of legs and feet. No one moved except to use the bucket.

Wind whistled right through the boxcar's many cracks and small openings, but its sturdy sides prevented any breakouts. Not that anyone would be foolish enough to set out on his own in the dead of a north Poland winter. We each had two German Army blankets in which we were bundled all of the time because the temperature was never above freezing, at least for the first few days. I remember those blankets smelled like straw, especially when they got a little damp. But the smell that I'm sure we all remember the best (or should I say the worst) is that of our bucket/latrine.

We subsisted on the Red Cross food parcels issued before we left Stettin because on the train trip we received no German food. All of the food in the parcels could be eaten without cooking, and was supposed to last one person one week. As it turned out our train trip lasted nine days, but we expended so little energy sitting in the boxcar that the one parcel was enough. Once a day the German guards gave us each half of a one-pound coffee can of water. Water was precious, and nobody washed. The train started and stopped a lot on the trip; sometimes the train sat on a rail siding for a couple of days.

We ate no fresh fruits or vegetables, and we were aware of the ever-present danger of infection from the slightest scratch. In the semi-darkness of the boxcar it wasn't so noticeable, but when we completed our journey and came out into the sunlight I was appalled to see how men had infected sores on their hands, arms, and faces.

At dusk of the third day the train entered the Berlin railroad complex. When the train came to a stop we figured we'd be there for the night. Everyone was asleep at about ten o'clock when the scream of air raid sirens jolted us awake. My heart pounded with fear, knowing that in that railroad yard we were sitting ducks for the RAF. At that point in the war, the RAF always bombed German cities at night. We heard the drone of aircraft and the explosion of many bombs. Then we heard several huge nearby explosions that turned out to be the firing of an anti-aircraft gun. Everyone shook in their boots waiting for a direct hit. With the acrid smell of smoke and dust in the air, the raid seemed to last forever. But after about half an hour the thunder of the bombs stopped, the drone of the bombers was gone, and the "all-clear" siren sounded.

We slept very little after that, because for all we knew the bombing might start again any time. Fortunately it didn't, and just before dawn our train rumbled out of the train yard and into the lowlands south of Berlin.

After liberation, three months later, I learned the U.S. Eighth Air Force sent thousands of bombers to Berlin the day we left, February 3rd. It was the biggest air raid of the war. The railroad yard was demolished.

Another event is burned into my memory of that miserable train trip. After we passed through Berlin, one of the prisoners in the boxcar ahead of ours developed a fever and became quite ill. The one medic on the train had nothing to give him but aspirin. He died that night with an aspirin still undissolved in his mouth. The following morning the train stopped in a peaceful countryside area and the man was carried on a makeshift stretcher to the top of a grassy knoll about a hundred yards from the train track. Under a cold overcast sky, about a half dozen of his buddies buried him while the rest of us watched through the cracks in the side of the boxcars. It was a very sad time. There was a lot of frustration and anger.

I experienced many sad as well as humorous incidents between November 2nd, 1944* and April 29th 1945,** but "The Train Trip" lingers indelibly in my memory.

*when my B-17 was shot down
**when we were liberated

John Wayne Wears a Girdle
by Grace Ferry

I'm scared to go into the principal's office. Any moment now the lady behind the desk will call my name and I'll have to go in. I know he's going to be angry. Once before, I was sent to him for calling a girl a bad name. She started it and it ended with me getting detention. I'm glad we don't have a phone. They can't call my mom. The office lady will give me a note to take home and I'll translate it for my mom who will look disappointed and give me the lecture about being a widow and not having my dad to help raise me. Oh, boy.

I want to tell you my side of the story and have you decide if that stupid George didn't deserve the punch in the nose. I save every penny I get my hands on. I sell bottles; run errands. I even don't buy the little boxes of chocolate milk at school. I save my money so I can go to the movies. My favorites are the cowboy movies and I love John Wayne. I make sure I have money for the bus and my ticket. If I'm lucky and my mom gives me a dime, I can buy a hot dog that comes in the foil bag that makes the bun warm and soft.

I love the Majestic Theater. It's beautiful. Two balconies, thick carpets, royal blue velvet curtains that open just before the movie starts and if you look up, there are twinkling lights in the ceiling that look like stars.

I don't like to sit in the balconies. That's where couples go to smooch. I also don't like to sit next to people who talk during the show. I find my seat, I curl my legs under me and I wait for the lights to go down and the movie to begin.

On Mondays we always ask each other, "did you go to the show?" We don't call them movies or films. If someone says, "I'm going to the show," we know what it means.

On Saturday afternoon I take the bus, buy my

ticket and sit by myself. Once the show starts I forget everything including that my dad died last year and that we have no money, and that the perm I got from my mom makes me look like a fat Shirley Temple. Sitting in the dark watching the show is heaven to me. Yes, I do love John Wayne. Not like you love a boyfriend but how you feel about someone who's good, kind and strong. I like him so much that I root for him even if it means the Mexicans get killed. I imagine John Wayne's kids are the luckiest in the world. He's tall, good-looking and brave. No one messes with him.

Now, let me tell you why I'm sitting here waiting for the principal. It wasn't my fault. Stupid George started it all.

"Hey Gorda, I saw you at the show on Saturday. Girls aren't supposed to like cowboy movies. What's wrong with you anyhow?"

I ignore him. I sit at my desk but I can still hear him telling other boys I like cowboy movies and they're all giggling. During lunch he comes over to bug me again.

"Hey Gorda, you're in love with John Wayne. You want to marry him."

"No I don't and you're just stupid."

"Then how come you tell everyone he's your favorite movie star?"

"Because he's the best and if you knew anything you would know that."

"Here's something you don't know. My sister read it in a movie magazine and it said that John Wayne wears a girdle."

Everyone in the lunchroom hears stupid George and they start laughing. I feel my face get hot and the next thing I know I have my fist in his face and blood is running out of his nose. The lunchroom lady runs over and puts a kitchen towel on his face and takes him away crying.

You know you're in trouble when the principal starts with, "well young lady."

"We sent George home with a bloody nose and now I want to know why you hit him?"

"He said something terrible to me. I didn't

mean to make his nose bleed. I just wanted him to stop saying those awful things."

A look of concern comes over Mr. Johnson's face. "What did he say to you to make you this upset that you had to hit him?"

"It's so awful I don't know if I can say it to you."

"Will you feel better telling Mrs. Brown and she can tell me?"

"No. It's a terrible thing no matter who I tell it to."

"What did George say to you? If it's truly that bad I will deal with him."

I put my hands over my face. I know I have to repeat those ugly words which have to be a lie. "John Wayne wears a girdle." I mumbled through my fingers.

"I'm sorry, but can you repeat that?"

"He said John Wayne wears a girdle." I repeated in a loud voice.

I break into tears. I'm not sure if it's because I'm still so angry or because I know I'm in trouble with the principal. Mr. Johnson comes from around his desk and hands me some Kleenex and touches my shoulder. For a moment I think I see the corner of his mouth curl up in a grin.

"I suppose you were very angry and felt you had to hurt him back."

I nodded.

"You know I can't have students hitting each other. No matter what. You can always come to me and I will take care of whatever is going on. I'm afraid you have to stay in detention for a week and write a note apologizing to George."

When I get home I hand my mom the note from the principal's office.

"Here," she hands it back to me, "tell me what it says."

I have to think fast. A new cowboy show is coming to the Majestic Theater on Saturday and I don't want to miss it. I read the note slowly and carefully.

Dear Mrs. Garcia,

This is to let you know that your daughter has volunteered to help after school for the next five days. She's a helpful girl and knows western history real well.

Sincerely,

The Principal

Sometimes even John Wayne is less than truthful.

Grandfather Clause
by Frank Warren

The Terms Grand and Great are meant to lend a dignity that "Old Coot" misses. Many grandfathers belong to societies such as the Neptune who offer a one-time only barbeque. Grandfathers' social lives often include meeting people with advanced degrees such as doctor. A visit to grandfather can bring groans and questions: "Do we have to listen again to how he shook hands with the mayor of Coalinga?" This grandfather refrains from mentioning how bright and optimistic his four granddaughters are. They and many like them may be the next "greatest generation."

Now if you've got a moment I'd like to tell you about shaking hands with the mayor of Coalinga.

The Cruise from Hell

by Robert A. Reid

The year was 1980 and the youngest of our four kids was five. My wife Patti's parents, Ed and Clara, agreed to come to Santa Barbara and babysit while we went on our first cruise. It was March and the cruise was a low-cost trip to the so-called Mexican Riviera and included a medical seminar on diabetes in pregnancy making it partially tax deductible.

The day of embarkation the whole family piled in the 1973 Ford Country Squire and drove to San Pedro to see us off. Everybody was allowed on the ship to check out the stateroom and have lunch and the kids were thrilled. I had upgraded our room to the top deck with a balcony but the bad news was that a lifeboat was obstructing our view out the sliding glass door.

Oh well, we thought, it is still an upgraded room. We went down to the swimming pool deck for lunch and what was the fare? Corndogs. Where was that great cuisine that cruise ships are supposed to have? The good news? You could have as many as you could eat. The kids were delighted.

At about four pm the ship was ready to sail. We said goodbye to the family, unpacked our suitcases and stowed our luggage. The refrigerator was stocked with beer and soft drinks so we grabbed a couple of beverages and ducked around the lifeboat to watch Los Angeles Harbor fade in the distance and the sun begin to set in the west. On this cruise dinner time and seating were assigned and ours was for six pm and we were seated with other doctors, their wives and some nurses totaling ten people. We were allowed in the dining room at precisely five-fifty-five and upon being seated all eight of our dining companions lit up cigarettes and smoked throughout the remainder of the meal. Our waiter, who I later found out was Indonesian, was surly and seemed quite bothered if you asked for anything special or for substitutions.

One of the choices for dinner was Chateaubriand with port wine reduction sauce so, despite the taste buds being ruined by cigarette smoke, I was looking forward to finally enjoying some elegant cooking. Alas when the pathetic piece of meat was served it was overdone and had a remarkable resemblance to the tongue of my shoe. Wine was extra, expensive and no way was I going to share any with these purported health professionals who weren't smart enough not to smoke. We asked to change tables but were told that we'd need to trade with someone else and, frankly, I was reluctant to ask anybody to take our place. Each night the menu changed and the meat was called something else. The next night it was roasted New York Steak, the following they called it Prime Rib, then Beef Tenderloin but on the plate was a cut of the same shoe leather that had been served the previous time. And then there was the ever present cigarette smoke.

Dinner had been a bit of an ordeal but we were on our way to the Mexican Riviera and our stateroom refrigerator was stocked with beer. Our television had a selection of movies so we stayed up late, watched a couple of features and got mildly buzzed. Falling asleep about two am we looked forward to getting up late. Alas, it was not to be. Our upgraded room was on an upper deck and right below a promenade where joggers began to stomp on the ceiling at five am.

Because of the short night and too much beer I was mildly hung over. The seas had become rough and we were a bit nauseated but prepared with Trans-Scope patches and put them on immediately. My medical seminar began at nine am and I was delighted to encounter Bob Phillips, one of my fellow obstetricians from Santa Barbara at the meeting. Unfortunately, I found that looking at slides about Diabetes in Pregnancy while the boat was rocking and rolling only

316

increased my nausea so I had to leave, return to my noisy stateroom and lie down. Four more days of this? My enthusiasm had died. Little did I know there was worse ahead.

Once the Scopolamine patch kicked in, I was able to get a nap and life seemed better. After a day at sea we arrived in Puerto Vallarta. The Princess Cruise ship on which they were actively filming "The Love Boat" was docked next to us and it was fun to watch the activity on deck. We had signed up for a catamaran trip down to Mismaloya Beach where the remains of the movie set, "Night of the Iguana" starring Ava Gardner and Richard Burton still remained. The weather was perfect, the sailing smooth and the Planter's Rum Punch was strong and plentiful. The captain anchored about 100 yards off the beach and announced that anyone wanting to go ashore would have to swim and be back on the boat within an hour. If you missed the boat, he suggested a cab back to the cruise dock.

Feeling strong, Phillips and I decided to go for

it. I jumped into the warm ocean and swam underwater as far as I could before coming up for air. I expected to be at least halfway to the sand when I surfaced but was shocked to be only about 20 yards from the boat's hull. So we swam and swam and swam until we both lay on the wet sand like a couple of shipwreck survivors. After lying there for a few minutes we decided to find and explore the movie set. Just then a horn went off from the catamaran and the captain waved for us to come back. We both dove in the surf and when we surfaced nearly hit our heads on the boat's hull. We had been victimized by a strong off-shore current on our way in and aided on the way back. It was a good thing because we neglected to take cab fare to the beach to pay for a long ride home.

Despite our foreshortened adventure on Mismaloya Beach, we found Puerto Vallarta with its cobblestone streets and walkable beachfront to be a charming port. They were filming "Love Boat" scenes on what is called the Malecon, a boardwalk and seawall along the beach. Our ship departed for Mazatlán after dinner and, while the sea was again a bit rough, our transdermal patches kept us dry-mouthed but well.

When on these medical seminar trips, I feel honor-bound to attend the lectures and the following morning there was more on diabetes in pregnancy. Unfortunately the speaker was poor, his graphics primitive and the rocking of the boat in the darkened room was threatening to break through my sea-sickness remedy. I went up on deck to get some fresh air and felt better. We were soon docked in Mazatlán so we disembarked to explore the city. We toured an ancient cathedral and the most impressive feature of the visit was a diminutive Mexican lady with a huge swelling on the front of her neck, obviously a goiter. I had never seen one before. There were many nice areas of the city but most memorable was Mazatlán General Hospital, a small building in a run-down neighborhood with all of its windows open and patients sitting on the sills trying to keep cool. Curtains were billowing in the wind and you had to wonder how anybody convalesced in such a place.

Since dinner was such a smoky ordeal on this cruise, we decided to eat in town. We read about a place called "The Shrimp Bucket" which was American- owned and used only filtered water to make ice, wash all their vegetables and dinnerware suggesting that by eating there you could avoid the infamous "turista" or gastroenteritis with diarrhea suffered by many gringos after dining in Mexico. This was good thinking on my part and the place was quite attractive with many appealing menu items. What was not good thinking was for me to order raw oysters which I love but are slightly risky to eat wherever you dine, but in Mexico, with the sanitation problems they had in 1980, was almost begging for trouble.

Not long after we returned to the ship, trouble came. My body rejected the obviously contaminated mollusks from both ends. The nausea returned with a vengeance and I was forced to sleep on the floor of our stateroom's head with the cool porcelain of the toilet as my pillow, something I had not done since my early days at college. Of course, even this episode only lasted until 5 am when the joggers began their daily stomp on our ceiling.

The night on the floor of the stateroom head with porcelain as a pillow was not restorative. Nausea and looseness persisted and there was no chance that I was going to grace the audience for the last session of "Diabetes in Pregnancy." That afternoon was to be our last port of call, Cabo San Lucas, so I pushed the Lomotil, Kaopectate and changed my Trans-Derm Scopolamine patch in an attempt to get well. Naturally, my wife, Patti although sympathetic to my condition, was not very pleased with the quality of her travel partner on this cruise.

Cabo San Lucas did not have a cruise ship dock at that time so the plan was to take groups to shore in tenders which are small boats holding about 30 passengers. Alas, the March seas were too rough to shuttle safely so we stood at the railing and stared longingly at the distant shore. Yet another disappointment among the many on this cruise.

At dinner that night, I could immediately tell that something was amiss. Our surly Indonesian waiter was smiling, calling us by name and offering to bring drinks and wine. He cheerfully served our portion of mystery meat, refilled our glasses and made pleasant small talk. I was totally confused as to what had brought about the change until, along with dessert, he passed out our cruise evaluation forms. He emphasized how important it was for him to receive a good evaluation to maintain his job and he hoped we would rate him four, the top ranking. I had no confusion about what ranking he deserved, nor did Patti and we scored him accordingly.

We sailed into San Pedro the next morning and this disaster was almost ended. We were both ready to disembark and drive home to Santa Barbara. Our luggage would meet us on the dock and we'd be off. Alas, on a very hot day with no shelter the luggage did not arrive. Apparently there was a problem with the ship's freight elevator and they were having to deliver it a piece at a time. By the time we loaded up the car and headed north we had reached the famed Los Angeles rush hour and had to endure the 405 freeway parking lot.

We looked back over our experience and several things stood out. Lousy food, lousy service, constant cigarette smoke, rough seas, sea sickness, disappointing shore excursions, little rest, no Cabo San Lucas and intolerable delay at disembarkation. Worst of all, I didn't learn a single new thing about diabetes in pregnancy.

It truly was the cruise from hell and it took us 20 years before we deigned cruise again and finally have a rewarding experience.

About the Authors

John M. Ackerman, M.D. is a retired psychiatrist who practiced in San Francisco (during the " Summer of Love", 1967) and in Alaska with the Indian Health Service before moving to Santa Barbara in 1970. He has contributed to two books on Subtle Energy Medicine. His family is grateful he has written these impressions.

Sharon Alvarado grew up in Santa Barbara, left and returned with stories to tell. She spent 50 years in the psychiatric field, 18 of which were in Santa Barbara. Sharon is the current leader of our Writer's Workshop. "Writing gives me permission to dream dreams, reveal secrets and walk in my own imagination."

Anna Lee Anderson was born in Long Beach, California of Chinese parents. She is very proud of the contributions of the Chinese to life on earth including silk, tea, noodles, porcelain, bamboo, sculpture, art, print, fortune cookies and writing from pictographs.

Rosita Arbagey was born in England into a military family and experienced World War II in London. She married an American oil executive in Singapore and lived in Karachi, Lahore Pakistan and Kabul Afghanistan. Later she was in The Hague, Istanbul and finally Cape Town, South Africa. Her adventures, of which she writes, are many and never fail to intrigue her fellow authors.

Joy Ehle's photographs and stories about her adventures in some of the wild places in the world have been published in *AAA Highroads, Ocean Magazine* and The *Santa Barbara Independent*. www/joyehle.com.

Grace De Soto Ferry was born in San Antonio, Texas in 1944. She's married to filmmaker John Ferry. They've been married forty-four years and have one son. She now lives in Santa Barbara, California. Grace has co-written and produced three documentaries. <u>Hey Guy, This is the Butterfly</u> and <u>Crows on the Line are her</u> first books of short stories.

Mary Frink, mother,
poet, postmaster and friend
loving grandmother

Barbara Godley, born in Santa Monica, now living in Summerland was a pre-school teacher in her earlier days. She is now active in League of Women Voters, Unity Church and takes a writer's workshop. She has two grown daughters, one granddaughter and two great grandchildren.

Douglas Huston says, "Writing for me is simply a fun way to share my particular glimpses of the universe and along the way tell my own story,"

Joan Jacobs has to write a short piece in a short time about herself. She ponders. Clock's ticking. Ponders some more. Tick. Tock. Tick. . . . . Time's up. Darn! (Last word needed?)

Gerson Kumin, a native of Washington D.C did not begin writing until after he retired. He now lives in Santa Barbara, California where he dreams of places far, far away and remains busy with his next masterpiece for class.

Bill Livingstone, a retired urban planner, was born in Los Angeles and has lived in the Santa Barbara area since 1977. He and his wife, Marge, enjoy writing their recollections and critiquing each other's work. Bill has written nearly 500 recollection pieces and over 100 fiction stories since he joined Joan Fallert's Writing and Recollecting class in 1991.

Marge Sweet Livingstone, a native of Iowa, has lived in California since 1946. Her career as a probate paralegal in Pasadena ended when she retired and moved to Goleta in 1999 where she and her husband Bill live in the Encina Royale seniors' community.

Joyce Metz says, "It has been 6 years since our class published its first book. Not much has changed in that time except our writing has gotten better – oh, and I've grown older, but I still haven't grown up."

Mead Northrop's first freshman English theme submitted at Hamilton College came back from his professor marked, "Gross illiteracy. See me." Mead has spent a lifetime trying to overcome his mortification. The writing class provided him with a pathway towards potential redemption.

Robert A Reid, as an obstetrician, attended over 5000 births in Santa Barbara; but has always had an abiding interest in writing after receiving an undergraduate degree in English Literature. He especially enjoys the fascinating stories that have emerged from the patients in his practice.

Margaret Roff has worked as a social worker,

special education teacher, at UCSB and for the City of Santa Barbara. After retiring, she asked her younger sisters if they remember their grandmother Maud. They said "no." So Margaret decided to attend a writing class to describe her.

Ken Rubenstein migrated from New Jersey to Silicon Valley in 1970 where he became a biotech researcher, manager, and consultant. Over 20 years he's written more than 40 book-length reports on new technology developments for sale to pharmaceutical and biotech companies. He's retired and enjoys creative writing.

Barry Shulman was born and lived in a California community before it became known as Silicon Valley. Raised three boys and had a career in the judicial system. Had the opportunity to travel and study abroad. Eventually moved to Santa Barbara County where he became an organic farmer and rancher. An empty nest and semi-retirement gave him some time to write. His poetry covers many facets of an adventurous life. The themes generally appear in the middle of the night and always rhyme.

Brian Silsbury - Startled, I awoke from a muse as the deep, sonorous voice echoed around my study walls. "Brian Silsbury, why did you move to Santa Barbara?"

Still shocked, I gathered my thoughts but only managed a few croaked sentences. "Work transferred me from the United Kingdom in 1995. Ten years later, I retired to Santa Barbara and joined a local writing group."

The voice persisted. "Why did you choose to write as a hobby?"

"What the hell has it to do with you?" I muttered under my breath.

"Tell me," the assertive voice demanded.

"Whatever the genre or 'voice', I gain enormous pleasure from creative writing and it is my hope my readers do too."

"Amen to that!" roared the voice as the echoing receded and finally fell silent.

Beth Thompson is a happily retired elementary school teacher who now has time and freedom to read, write, garden, play with her golden retriever, and practice yoga. The best part of her leisure is seeing her grandchildren and family. She enjoys her community of writers and sharing her life with amazing friends.

Frank Warren was a native of Nebraska, migrated to California as a teenager, served in World War II and then had a very successful career as a graphic artist. Lately Frank had been exploring his considerable talent as a writer. Frank passed away on September 13th, 2017. Prior to his death he had written the following: *"Each morning I walk with a walker around Rancho Santa Barbara. I encounter few fellow residents but I hope this effort stretches my glide toward the Big Sleep. Yesterday, the damndest thing happened: A human figure about eight-feet tall wearing a pointed helmet with metal wings on each side. This creature* *seemed to be a dark-skinned female of uncertain nationality and with biceps of immense size. Without warning she swept me and my walker into her arms. I complained that her helmet wings were a danger. She made a rumbling sound and carried me to my mobile home where she set me down. I felt a great relief and cheerily asked her name. She smiled expressing the whitest teeth I've ever seen. "I think you already know."*

Raven Wolfe grew up in Ohio and moved to Santa Barbara in 1972,before the tourists discovered it, when it was a quiet, laid back beach town where nothing started on time and no one seemed to care. She has been published. Writing is her passion.

Suzanne Yoast-Perko is a landscape painter now writing about the many adventures in her vagabond youth. She has three grown daughters and lives in Santa Barbara with her husband Bob.

Made in the USA
San Bernardino, CA
04 August 2018